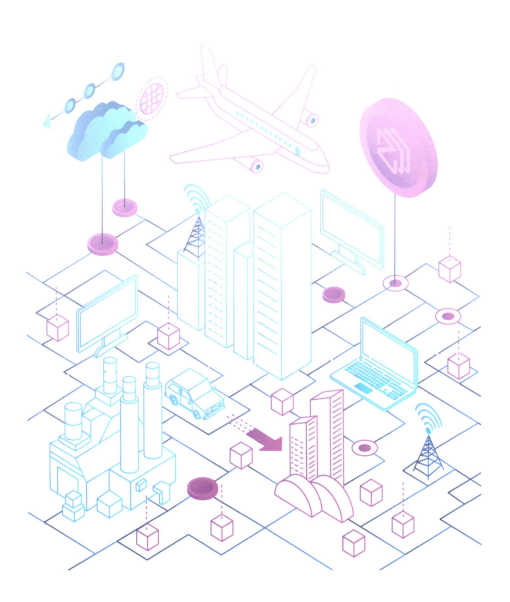

New Strategies in Blockchain

Volume 1

Authored by
Barton Johnston and Roberto Capodieci,
with the help of Stefano Griggio

Published by:

Version 1.2 P

ZooBC: New Strategies in Blockchain

Copyright © 2021 BCZ Holding Company Limited, Hong Kong.

ISBN: 978-1-7349179-0-1 (Paperback)
ISBN: 978-1-7349179-1-8 (Hardcover)
ISBN: 978-1-7349179-2-5 (Video Card Edition)
ISBN: 978-1-7349179-3-2 (Kindle)
ISBN: 978-1-7349179-4-9 (PDF)
ISBN: 978-1-7349179-5-6 (Google Live Doc)

Any references to forks, 51% attacks, historical events, real people, or real places are used accurately. Names, characters, and places are products of reality.

Printed by printing companies in various locations, including Hong Kong, China, Singapore, and Indonesia.

First printing edition 2021

BCZ Holding Company Limited
13/F LKF 29 NO 29 Wyndham St.
Central
Hong Kong

www.zoobc.com

This is the non-technical table of contents, for the technical contents see page 22

The Human Side

We dedicate this book, and the thousands of hours of technical and business work it represents, to the decentralized future, and especially to the vision of Satoshi Nakamoto.

Acknowledgements

No new idea comes out of nowhere. It is always inspired by problems encountered in the real world. For this reason, in a certain way, we are grateful to the many clients and projects we had experience with, whose visions helped us realize what is possible with blockchain technology, and what is missing in order to get there. We would like to thank everyone we have consulted for, and who has consulted with us, for participating in the great brainstorming and conception that led to the design of ZooBC technology, without whom we could never have created such a technology in a vacuum.

Additionally, none of this would have been possible without the help and support of the full team of Blockchain Zoo, who have worked tirelessly for nearly two years to execute the implementation and presentation of ZooBC technology; and our advisors, who have always been present to provide feedback and ideas, with whom we had endless disscusions on decentralization and cryptography.

Thank you everyone for your part in our small contribution to the future of blockchain!!

Roberto Capodieci

Barton Johnston

Foreword

Since the rise of Bitcoin into popular conception, there has undeniably been a lot of activity in the blockchain space. New projects rise and fall, novel ideas are debated and discarded, huge funding is raised and spent. Hopes have been raised the world over for new paradigms in information systems to emerge and solve the longstanding problems of trust and transparency that have come to characterize the conventional Internet.

Until today, most of these remain only hopes, not fully realized solutions. The world still awaits for the day when blockchain makes good on its implicit promise to transform our world into a better place.

As a professor, I have kept a close watch on the activity in this field, with passionate interest.

It is an unfortunate reality that for every one blockchain project which takes some substantive step forward, there are ten which stand still or even lose ground, and perhaps a hundred which only hoped to raise funding on false promises which were always intended to be squandered. This is not necessarily unexpected. Perhaps any nascent technology which is so poorly understood, and which so easily lends itself to the promise of quick riches, should attract such an array of characters, including charlatans alongside the more honest and genuine practitioners.

We do not wish to discourage anyone who has an interest in pursuing a career or considering a startup in blockchain. On the contrary, there is no better time since the value of blockchain projects has become a lot more apparent given the social distancing brought about by the Covid-19 pandemic. What is interesting is that those projects that are going from strength to strength are the ones that address the secure distribution of trust and those that serve the underserved. The talents behind these projects not only have a better understanding of what the technology is capable of doing, combining with their sense of mission, but they also seem to be thriving and gaining traction in this second wave of growth.

Despite a massive and unproductive amount of noise and churn, and millions of invested dollars burned on the same, there are still many intelligent people working relentlessly to pursue their goals, especially on the technical front. This effort takes the form of a collection of meaningful projects, each of which represents some incremental step forward. By these steps, we gradually learn over time which formulations and algorithms are actually secure, efficient, and practical to achieve the secured distribution of trust. All these are possible by learning from our own and the mistakes of others. The highest flight of human wisdom is the admission that the only thing we can know is that we know nothing, except to continuously observe the purity of intention and the sense of mission.

In this spirit, I would like to introduce the ZooBC project.

There are certainly large problems that stand in the way of making blockchain conducive to widespread adoption: unlimited scalability, general computation and storage, full user privacy, legal ramifications of digital representation of physical objects, and many others.

Unfortunately, in the "gold rush" to find solutions to these large issues, many have stopped short of taking the time to address some of the more obvious sharp corners of the technology.

Some of the things standing in the way of blockchain's adoption are not so grandiose: how long must you wait for the blockchain history to download on your computer? How much hard drive space must you allocate to facilitate the eventual unlimited growth of the data? What is a node operator's realistic chance of being rewarded in tokens for having served the network?

ZooBC has its own unique vision for how to address the aforementioned large problems in the long term. This is true of many projects and by itself is not noteworthy. But ZooBC's architects have also recognized that it is not necessary to solve every large problem on day one to make a meaningful contribution to the evolution and adoption of blockchain.

Therefore, in the first version of the ZooBC blockchain technology, they have focused on addressing the lesser problems described above, along with many others. At the same time, in building this technology from scratch, their architectural choices have been made with a vision toward the future, developing a foundational framework on which future incremental releases of their technology may build to reach solutions to the big problems.

Even if only the smaller goals were achieved, this is meaningful work. Operating a blockchain has a lot of room to become less painful, and companies or institutions are slow to pick up a technology that is painful to work with.

In this way, ZooBC, even in its first version, may increase the usability and reputation of blockchain in general; if nothing else, it will yield more information about what kinds of approaches can be tried and how they will work in the real world, knowledge of which the team is sure to incorporate into their future work.

With this presentation of a few new solutions to real problems comes the hope that the architects of ZooBC will make good on their future promise to propose and implement new strategies to address the truly large obstacles blockchain faces. Although we only see teasers of such solutions in this paper, I am confident that through the success of this first phase of the ZooBC project we will all have the opportunity to see how much further its architects and engineers are able to go in their next round of designs.

The team from Blockchain Zoo, and in particular Mr. Roberto Capodieci, have been regular participants at the Singapore University of Social Sciences (SUSS) FinTech and Blockchain Group events. Roberto conducted the "Distributed Tic-Tac-Toe" at the university and has been a SUSS fellow since 2016. ZooBC has played an important role in preparing our students for the new digital economy, of which blockchain is a major driver, and the Fourth Industrial Revolution, and essential subjects in our bachelor and masters' degrees.

I wish Blockchain Zoo the best in their project!

- David LEE Kuo Chuen
Professor, Singapore University of Social Sciences

Preface

We are encouraged by the fact that Frankenstein has been indeed a successful story, book and movie, as our work has pretty much followed a similar path: born as reference material, grew into a white paper, to then become an experimental book from the future, to enlighten the few that are working on the lower technical levels to make decentralization technology strong, fast, and reliable.

The ZooBC project, like its white paper, has been an ever growing and changing entity, as we continue to develop new ideas and designs, imagine new use cases and work to support them, and learn from ongoing events with existing blockchain technologies. It was not something that started with a single purpose and stopped at that purpose; rather, at any point in time, it is the reflection of everything we have learned, and even though we must release a version in a single state for the network to reach consensus, our work will continue into developing new versions and integrating new designs and technologies in an effort to ultimately reach the pinnacle of what is possible with blockchain.

Blockchain Zoo, as a company, has had a similar trajectory. We have orbited around the need to bring new intelligence and insight into the world of blockchain, which concretely took many different iterations and concurrent attempts, including creating a decentralized association of blockchain professionals, running a blockchain technology consultancy, running a blockchain software development service, launching public information campaigns about advanced blockchain features, opening a Blockchain-centric co-working space in our blockchain Zoo offices, and now developing from scratch and releasing a novel blockchain technology.

It is not an accident that our paths have been so convoluted and circular: Blockchain itself is new, poorly understood, and certainly operating below its potential as a technology to transform the internet and the world. New developments, steeped in mysterious mathematics, cryptography, and architecture, appear every day, and must be absorbed, discerned, polished, explained, and ultimately included into our work. Of these modern developments, in our first release of the ZooBC blockchain, we have touched more than most, but fewer than we would like; our passion for capturing them all in one platform that can serve the future of blockchain will carry us down yet more winding roads to discover where there is gold and where there is none.

As you read this book, you will see artefacts of the long and winding road we have taken from the birth of Blockchain Zoo to the launch of ZooBC technology, and our projections of the maps ahead. We have attempted to condense some small part of this complicated story, and the fruits of our constant work and refinement over the last 3 years, into this book. Surely, if this book was published another one year or two from now (which we intend to do in a second volume), it would be entirely different in character and content again. So, rather than taking this book as the final word on Blockchain Zoo and ZooBC, we hope you will see it as a moment on a long journey, and we invite you to join us in making that journey together toward the future of blockchain!

Book Highlights

April 2020 - After years of building custom blockchains (with customized consensus rules, special transaction types, etc). We listed all of the pain points we would have loved to see addressed on a new blockchain platform and then decided to build it. After almost two years of work, with a team of 25 dedicated developers, we now have a beta version of ZooBC running on a public testnet (we plan to open source ZooBC and launch the main net in March 2021).

Some of the innovations we have developed in ZooBC are as follows:

● Compliance

Transactions can be signed with government-issued digital signatures

Accounts can refuse/accept incoming transactions

❯ Read about accounts at page 47

Native blockchain objects (digital twins)

Accounts can create blockchain objects (items with fix/editable data and properties attached)

Blockchain objects can change ownership, be transferred, updated, sold, etc.

> *Read about digital twins at page 51*

Native escrowed transactions

Automated with centralized services (easily creates a decentralized exchange)

Human managed (for example, the execution of title transfers can be authorized by a notary)

> *Read about escrowed transactions at page 62*

Cryptographic multisig

Transactions can be prepared both on-chain and off-chain

Works hierarchically

Works natively with escrowed transactions

> ❯ *Read about multisig at page 83*

Liquid transactions

Send funds continuously (per minute / per hour) with a max total amount that can be set

The transaction can be stopped by the sender, receiver, or escrowed by a 3rd party

> ❯ *Read about liquid transactions at page 66*

ZooBC runs on a Raspberry Pi

Can be ported to run on a cellphone

Everyone can easily run a node

> *Read about creating snapshots*
> *at page 165*

The code is simple

Written for everyone to customize it

Well documented

It is easy to create with, and on top of, ZooBC

> *Request access to GitHub repository*
> *here: https://bcz.bz/gitrepo*

Native distributed data storage

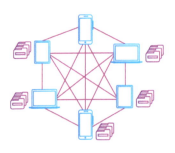

Data is stored in a subset of nodes, with enough redundancy

Now only used for blocks and snapshots (see below)

In future versions of ZooBC will be used for transaction attachments also

Snapshots

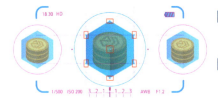

Once a month the current state of the blockchain is snapshotted

Nodes can download snapshots and rebuild the state of the blockchain at various point in time

Snapshots can be cryptographically validated without downloading the whole blockchain

> *Read about snapshots at page 165*

A shortcut to any point of the blockchain

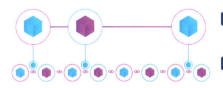

Special blocks (we call them spine blocks) are created one per day

Spine blocks are cryptographically locked from the genesis block to the current height

Spine blocks contain minimal data (no transactions)

Nodes can use spine blocks as a shortcut to reach a snapshot

> *Read about spine blocks at page 155*

New nodes up and running in less than 1 hour

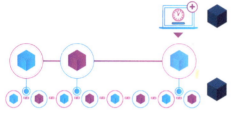

Thanks to spine blocks and snapshots a new node is up to date in a short time

No matter how old the blockchain is, the space in a node HDD remains manageable (2mb of data)

❯ *Read about joining the network at page 107*

Scalability (through multi chains and infra-chains transactions)

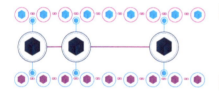

The base technology to implement this function is already present in V1 of ZooBC

In future versions of ZooBC:

- *Spine blocks will offer a shortcut to more than one chain*
- *Multiple chains will run sharing the same spine blocks*
- *it will be possible to make transactions between chains*

❯ *Read about spine block at page 155*

⦿ Decentralized applications (in next version)

Not smart contracts, but full running applications

Subsets of nodes can run specific applications

ZooBC can guarantee an application-specific consensus

As you may have notice, we are introducing a lot of innovations to the blockchain world, but the core of what we have done with ZooBC is introducing a new blockchain consensus model that we call Proof of Participation. Please bear with me through this explanation, as it is fundamental to our work: Blockchain was originally created to support decentralized digital money, and the way a blockchain is secured (the consensus model, the heart of how each node chooses which blockchain to follow in the case of a fork) is essentially based on the value of the blockchain "coin" or "token". This is OK when the core function of the blockchain is merely to manage its own token. In the current paradigm, a blockchain is secure as long as its token is sufficiently valuable, but it becomes a security risk when the blockchain is used for non-financial cases (medical records management, know your customer(KYC), etc.) where there is no reason for the token to hold a high value, or when a blockchain with a valuable token is used to manage titles with a value larger than the full blockchain economy/market cap. This applies to Proof of Work, Proof of Stake, and most, if not all, other consensus mechanics.

ZooBC's Proof of Participation establishes a trusted peer-to-peer network of nodes, some of which gain the right, by consensus rules, to be part of a registry. Nodes in the registry are entitled to verify transactions, create new blocks, and share among them the coinbase reward of new coins generated at every new block. The time interval at which a single new node can join the registry gets smaller as the registry gets bigger. With 1,000 nodes in the registry, a new node is accepted every 8 hours, for an average of 3 new nodes per day. As the registry gets bigger, the time interval for new nodes to join shortens, whereas if many nodes leave or are kicked out of the registry, the time interval grows. This is done as a layer in the security of the blockchain, to make it difficult for someone to suddenly have a large percentage of the nodes in the registry and perform an attack. Nodes in the registry maintain a participation score calculated by their actual participation in maintaining the blockchain network. Failing or refusing to participate (a node goes offline, does not update the core software, etc). will result in a degrading of the participation score, and thus less sharing of coinbase rewards, until the score hits zero and the node is removed from the registry. Proof of Participation detaches the security of the blockchain from the tokens or coins usually used as the means to safeguard a blockchain. Measuring actual work (participation) to keep the network alive allows adoption of blockchain technology by business models that do not need the use of a cryptocurrency, such as a consortium of hospitals that wants to manage medical records, government offices that need to control documentation flows, etc. With a blockchain based on Proof of Participation, they will have a secure and strong network without the need to worry about a coin value.

It is worth to noting that when our blockchain is deployed with a core coin, the transaction fees collected and the coinbase reward are distributed between all the nodes in the registry: both those that create new blocks and those that just validate transactions. This motivates all the nodes to always be present and do their job. In comparison other blockchains, from Bitcoin up, give the reward only to the nodes that successfully create new blocks, but no rewards are given to the nodes that do the very important work of confirming the validity of new blocks and new transactions. The cost for those nodes, Internet connection, electricity bills, and hardware maintenance, has to be paid by the node owner on a voluntary basis.

So, the core part of Proof of Participation is how to prove that nodes are actually doing work to keep a robust and stable P2P network. We explored many models, did extensive tests, simulated attack methods, and more. We cannot rely on nodes' "opinions" of other nodes' behavior, as that is an attack vector that is easily exploitable and cannot be objectively proven. We needed something that, from the genesis block, could be traced, telling us which subset of nodes was authoritative in proposing new blocks, what their participation score was, and how the network's attitude about them changed over time, without taking much space on the blockchain.

To accomplish this, we implemented a receipt system. In short, key elements of the P2P data traffic are used as a means to show that the data transited through a node. A node that receives data can digitally sign a receipt and send it back to the originating node. If that data ends up leaving a mark in the blockchain, that receipt shows valid work done. Merkel roots of receipts are saved in the blocks, and when a node recognizes its data, it can claim (by showing the receipt - that it did the work, getting the score assigned to it.

Here is a video that illustrates the process:
How Receipts in ZooBC Work

Abstract

Since the unfolding of Bitcoin, a plethora of blockchain technologies has emerged, each approaching certain limitations of the original design. In the same spirit, in the first of what we intend to be a sequence of gradual improvements, in this paper we propose a new blockchain architecture and generally describe its structure. Among other aspects, we focus on a more evenly distributed block creation, a fair distribution of the network rewards among the nodes that do useful work for the network, a reduced blockchain download time that, no matter how bloated the blockchain is, remains a constant, and the creation of a flexible technological base upon which others may implement the business logic specific to their domain. To start we explore the security and performance implications of each new blockchain and, where those differ from ZooBC, our blockchain technology.

Disclaimer

This version of *ZooBC: New Strategies in Blockchain* originated as a snapshot in time of the ZooBC white paper: a constantly evolving and living document. The long-term vision for ZooBC is planned over 10 years, with a new release of ZooBC every 2 years. Together with each new release of ZooBC, we aim to release a new volume of the 5 planned volumes in this collection of "New Strategies in Blockchain". Enjoy the read and help with insights, comments, questions, and suggestions using the book's online interactive pages by following the QR codes you can find throughout the book. Together we will pave the road for a next-generation blockchain and a decentralized future!

> **NOTE:** *The Proof of Existence (PoE) of the PDF version of this book can be found at this URL: **https://bcz.bz/vol1poe**, and the PDF used for the Proof of Existence can be downloaded from this URL: **https://bcz.bz/vol1***

Privacy Considerations

Before looking at the structure of ZooBC V1, we should address an important point. Moving into the future of blockchain and decentralized systems, there is increasing concern over the entirely-public nature of the data on the blockchain. While privacy in ZooBC is simply handled with data encryption, other forms of privacy management, such as zero proof transactions, will be implemented in ZooBC V2, and they stand out clearly in our minds as important to address in the technology as a whole. **In Appendix 2, we list the thoughts that are guiding us as we begin designing V2 of the ZooBC blockchain technology.**

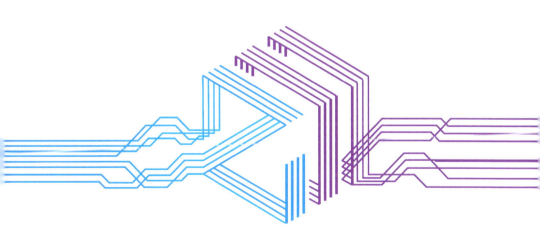

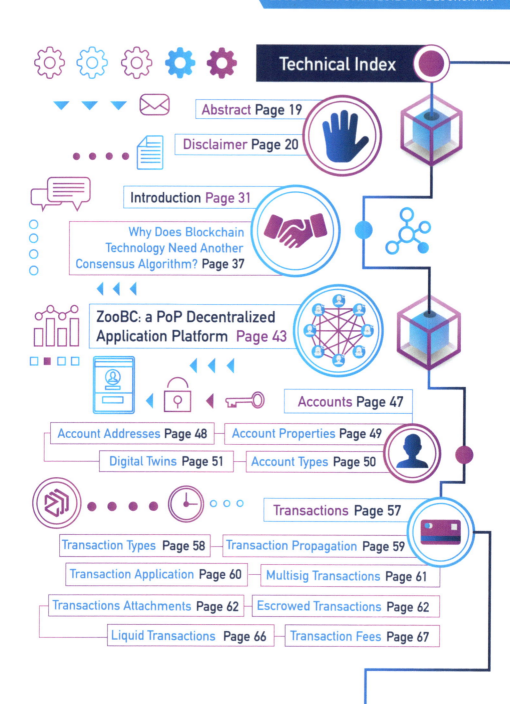

Technical Index

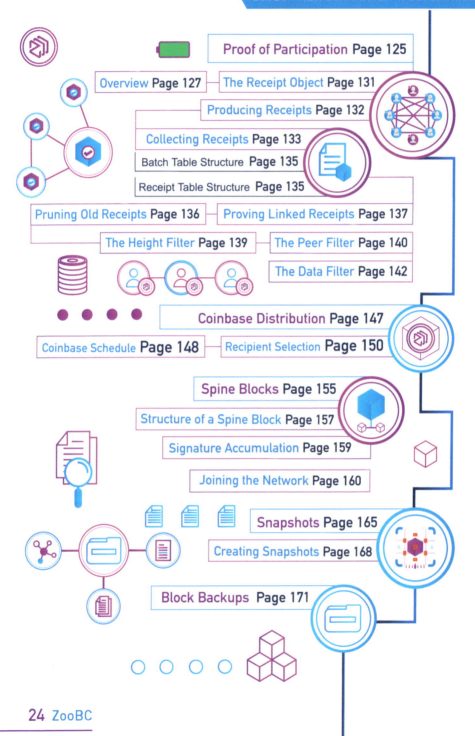

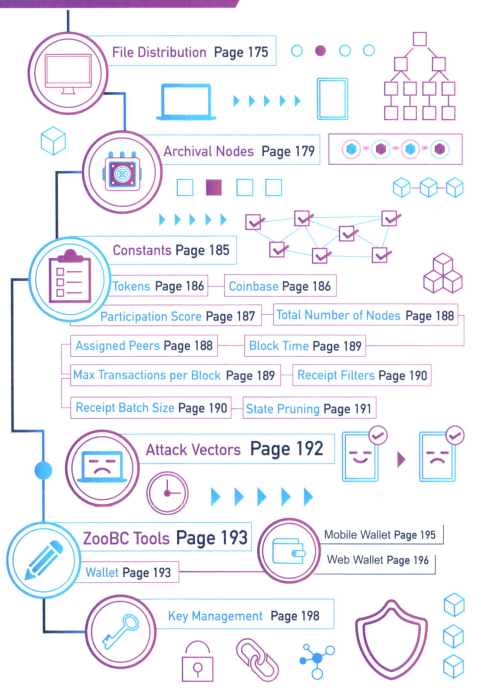

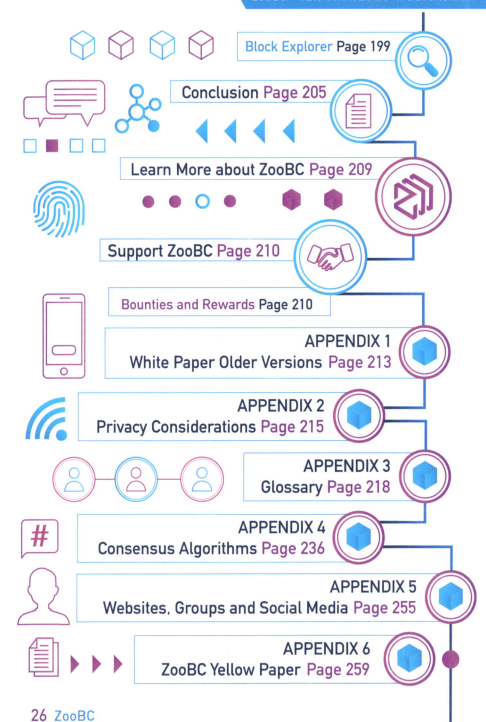

Do We Really Need Another Blockchain Protocol?

1.bcz.bz/3m
Interact

Scan to discuss this
chapter online

Let's look at the problem another way: what problems does a blockchain really solve, if any? And what needs to change in the technology for it to do those tasks better than what we have already?

To answer those questions, we need to understand what a blockchain is, and isn't. In its simplest form, a blockchain is a database: a store of data. But it's where that data is stored, and how it's accessed, that is the key. There are fundamental differences between an ordinary database and a blockchain, and it's those differences that persuade its supporters that a blockchain could change the way we exchange, store, process, and access data. Blockchain doesn't solve a technology problem, it solves a human problem: the problem of trust.

It does this by not relying on a single person, company, organization, or government to manage and control that data. Think about how the world works now: money changes hands as digits in a bank's server; your medical data is stored on the computers of hospitals, doctors, and insurers; if you have bought a house you'll know all the gatekeepers involved: real estate agent, insurance company, conveyancer, valuer, pest- and building inspectors, lender, finance broker, and if you're in a chain transaction the number of parties.

This works if you trust all those involved in the transaction, or who are holding your data. But trust is not something we can easily measure. How much do you trust your bank with your data? How do you measure whether you can trust a piece of information on a website or a financial advisor recommended to you by a friend of a friend? Oftentimes, we use third parties to flag whether something or someone is trustworthy: a certificate issued by an association or the government, a bank whose brand we recognize.

But this trust comes with a cost. The most obvious cost is the toll exacted: that certificate costs money to attain, and that cost will be passed on to you in legal fees, for example. The bank whose brand you feel you can trust? That branding has a price, as do the premises and staff that help to promote it. At the very least, you pay for that trust in transfer and other banks fees for every transaction, or for merely storing your money in their computers. Another cost is that you have to agree to their terms so that the bank, for example, can decide when you can make a transfer, or when an institution can confirm a certificate's authenticity. The cost of trust also means the bank effectively controls your money, determines who you can transfer money to, and even whether you may have a bank account at all. At the very least, you may find that you send money overseas on a weekend.

Part of blockchain's appeal is that it does away with much of this need for trust. In the cases above, because the trust is not baked into the institution, then so long as the blockchain network is working, then the transaction can happen. The bank is now no longer the arbiter of trust and effectively controlling the account in your name. That role is no longer necessary because with a blockchain there is no need for trust. Some people talk of a 'trustless' blockchain, but it isn't exactly that. A blockchain has taken over the role of what we think of as trust. It's not that we no longer need to trust those we transact with, but that we don't need a third party to be the arbiter. The blockchain does it for us: we don't need a third party to provide the rails for any transaction, we don't need a third party to give us confidence that our money is in safe hands, because we can monitor it transparently on the blockchain, and we don't need to hold funds in escrow with a third party because that can be handled by the blockchain. The transaction is trustless because we don't need a third party. That makes the transaction simpler, cheaper, and more transparent.

So why aren't we already doing this? Part of the problem is that we still haven't fixed some key problems with blockchain. This isn't surprising. Blockchain itself is the culmination of decades of thinking and tinkering in a range of technologies, disciplines, and research to solve one of the digital world's thorniest problems: how can you build a digital system in a world where copying something is as easy as a keyboard command like Command+C or a mouseclick, which everyone can trust to work, but where users don't have to trust anyone involved, or one or more entities to manage it?

We are long-time disciples of blockchain but have found in more than 5 years of consulting that there's a key gap between the needs of businesses interested in adopting blockchain and the technology itself. Sometimes those gaps can be overcome with tweaks and surgery, but these alterations often undermine the value of using blockchain in the first place or make the process unwieldy or insecure. In one case, for example, every tweak to the bespoke blockchain we made for one client ran up against the client's lawyers.

And in many cases we had to just say no: we advised our clients that blockchain wasn't the best solution to their problem because it just wasn't suitable. Blockchain can't solve every problem; it's not a magic bullet. We ended up walking away from one contract because we knew that blockchain wasn't the right solution for them; a simple database would have worked better and more cheaply.

These experiences forced us to confront a problem: for all its progress, and all the smart people working on it, blockchain technology needed fixing. So, while the rest of the world whipped itself into a frenzy over blockchain, inflating a speculative bubble in initial coin offerings, we retreated to our lab in deepest Bali. We ignored all the hubbub, and instead focused on addressing the core issues we felt blocked block-chain from realizing its full potential, and eventually came up with a new blockchain protocol we call ZooBC.

Introduction

As blockchains have grown from Bitcoin into a multitude of diverse technologies, a few key problems have remained largely unsolved. Many technologies take different approaches to ameliorate some of the issues, but some remain unaddressed, and many others remain unsatisfactorily solved. In the first version of our proposed technology, we do not aim to address all of them, but address some, and lay a foundation to address others. A few such issues are these:

Consensus algorithms are still evolving rapidly. Broadly, consensus algorithms of existing blockchains fall into three categories: **scarcity of external resources (such as Proof of Work), scarcity of internal resources (such as Proof of Stake), and federated consensus models.** The first two derive their security from who has the most money, which is a weak security model for a blockchain where the objects of interest are non-financial; most federated models make security compromises around how members are elected to, or ejected from, the federation.

Blockchains typically do not reward the nodes which do meaningful work for the network. Most chains reward only those nodes which create the blocks but do not have a method to measure which nodes are gossiping messages and thereby keeping the network decentralized. This is largely because it is not easy to achieve consensus on the behavior of so many nodes in a trustless, decentralized way. However the obvious problem remains: a perfectly efficient actor will learn to create blocks but not gossip transactions.

Blockchains download slowly, and the length of the download depends on the age and activity level of the chain. In many cases, such as Bitcoin or Ethereum, the chain becomes so large that it is a large investment or undertaking to even join the network to operate a node. The difficulty for a new node to join the network makes it challenging for networks to grow large enough to have the true robustness of decentralization.

Decentralized applications running on blockchains are currently restricted to either being strongly-coupled, such as smart contracts which may only be coded in the blockchain's language in a limited environment, or weakly-coupled, such as external pseudo-centralized applications which read and write important data to the blockchain as a storage layer. There is a lot of room between these extremes to be explored, to allow the creation of decentralized applications which leverage the decentralized network of the blockchain and its security properties, while not being bound entirely into a sandbox where each instance merely replicates the results of the others.

The ZooBC Project as a whole aims to analyze, experiment, and ultimately develop solutions to these and other problems facing the ecosystem of blockchain technologies.

Project Goals

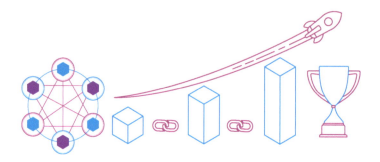

Our long-term vision with the **ZooBC** project is to develop a public, scalable, decentralized application platform and also to create a core blockchain technology that can be easily adapted to other business use cases for private deployments. With ZooBC V2.0, which will be the subject of a later white paper, Blockchain Zoo is developing an approach toward decentralized applications ("DApps") which is radically different from the conventional "smart contracts" approach used by Ethereum and other blockchain technologies. However, before working toward this goal, we have elected to start with ZooBC V1.0, a more conservative technology that lays the foundation for future work.

1.bcz.bz/22
Interact

This first version is similar to other existing blockchain technologies but with a few extra key core mechanics which will be leveraged more thoroughly as ZooBC progresses into future versions. These core functions bring some unique value to the first version of ZooBC but will deliver vastly more as new functionalities, such as the **DApp platform, geo scalability**, and **infra-chain transactions**, are implemented (more on this in V2 of the white paper).

1.bcz.bz/23
Interact

The first major diversion from previous blockchain technologies is a new consensus algorithm called **Proof of Participation** that has been architected, engineered, and implemented by Blockchain Zoo. In the context of the DApp platform that will be ZooBC V2.0, the Proof of Participation algorithm gives ZooBC a large consensus-tracked set of participating nodes with incentives to remain online, which can later be organized into sub-federations that may perform more efficient consensus algorithms for DApps. In the following pages, we develop the motivation for pursuing a new kind of algorithm and show how its design logically follows from the development of previous popular consensus algorithms.

1.bcz.bz/24
Interact

The second major diversion from previous blockchains is the use of a lightweight cryptographic shortcut made of special blocks created once per day, called *"spine blocks"*. This secures the state of the ZooBC blockchain at certain checkpoints and allows new nodes to identify and download the latest state of the network, cryptographically secured, without having to download and apply all the previous blocks and transactions.

In the context of a DApp platform, this checkpointing system can be used to secure the state of many apps, or even many blockchains, in one single place. For this first version of ZooBC, its utility is limited to enabling new nodes to safely and quickly join the network at the current state.

1.bcz.bz/25
Interact

The third major diversion from previous blockchains allows a user to choose which digital signature algorithm will secure his account and to configure an account so that it requires approval to receive transactions. These changes are targeted at increasing the blockchain's compatibility with various government regulations, for example using digital signatures recognized in court to validate blockchain transactions and proving a user agreed to receive certain funds or assets before they are attributed to his ownership.

1.bcz.bz/26
Interact

This paper will discuss in more detail the first release of the ZooBC technology (ZooBC V1.0 and enhancements toward the V2.0). **For a better understanding of the blockchain terminology used in this paper, please refer to the glossary in Appendix 3 at page 218.**

Why Does Blockchain Technology Need Another Consensus Algorithm?

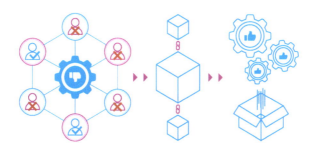

To understand why we have opted to implement novel mechanics to secure our blockchain, this section offers an overview of various existing consensus algorithms. This is for those readers wanting a more detailed account of the history of consensus algorithms and the reasons why we thought it necessary to develop beyond existing work. For those wanting to go straight to ZooBC's specifications and technical details, only the "Proof of Participation" paragraph is relevant.

1.bcz.bz/27
Interact

The blockchain space is saturated with attempts to improve efficiency, security, and fairness in the way that nodes reach a consensus on the history of events witnessed by the network. While the explosion of strategies may seem overwhelming or unnecessary, each project (some more than others) is doing its part in exploring the properties and tradeoffs yielded by each approach, and the crypto community is collectively narrowing down the proposed consensus strategies Darwinistically, until only the strongest are left standing.

1.bcz.bz/28
Interact

Here's a brief overview of the major approaches to blockchain consensus, and our reasoning to claim Blockchain Zoo's Proof of Participation as an improvement over its predecessors. **For a more detailed overview and visualization, please see Appendix 4 at page 236.**

Proof of Work Consensus

The Bitcoin white paper introduced the concept of using accumulated "Proof of Work" as a method for any node to agree on which blockchain, among forks, should be trusted. This approach was very powerful  because it allowed nodes to independently and objectively agree on one proposed history of events among many alternatives, in a way that resists a *"Sybil attack"* (because votes are counted by CPU cycles, not by accounts). While many insist that Proof of Work is still the safest way to secure a blockchain, time has shown some undesirable properties of the algorithm, such as increasing energy usage, centralization of the mining power, and the potential for externalized control. **Find out more about PoW in Appendix 4 at page 236.**

1.bcz.bz/29
Interact

Proof of Stake Consensus

These concerns motivated some to develop an alternate consensus algorithm to objectively choose between proposed versions of the blockchain history called "Proof of Stake".

In this approach, the likelihood of a network participant adding a block to the history is computed according to how many tokens on the network she possesses, and the block she creates is proven to originate from her via a digital signature. In this way, which chain required "more work" to create is simulated by a calculation of which nodes added blocks at which times and their relative stakes. This design requires minimal energy and guarantees that, in a fork, the nodes will choose the blockchain created by the majority of highly-invested network participants - in other words, those who have a larger stake of tokens locked to create new blocks. However, this strategy still has some undesirable properties such as a majority of the tokens being in the hands of only a few participants, and the possible creation of an alternate blockchain history controlled by only a small number of private keys. **Find out more about PoS in Appendix 4 at page 236.**

1.bcz.bz/2a
Interact

Federated Consensus

These consensus algorithms have been well-studied long before the emergence of blockchain technology for use in other distributed systems. While we feel such strategies effectively address the concerns above, in other ways they are a step backward from Proof of Work and Proof of Stake. Federated networks are no longer "permissionless", and the set of federated entities is usually well known, so we feel a pure federation is not acceptable for secure decentralized consensus. **Find out more about Federated Consensus in Appendix 4 at page 236.**

1.bcz.bz/2b
Interact

Delegated Proof of Stake Consensus

One of the most popular modern approaches to improving the scale of a blockchain network is to use *"Delegated Proof of Stake"* Consensus, where the accounts of the blockchain vote, with their stake, for a small number of nodes running large enough hardware to become block creators and thus support a high transaction volume blockchain. While this approach can dramatically increase the throughput of the network, it does so at the expense of decentralization, having similar flaws as conventional Proof of Stake and small federations (as described above). Specifically, these are the ease of quickly collecting enough stake to control the network, and the ability of a small number of block creators to conspire to censor transactions. **Find out more about DPoS in Appendix 4 at page 236.**

1.bcz.bz/2c
Interact

Byzantine Fault Tolerant Consensus

Another popular strategy for increasing the transaction throughput of a decentralized network is an algorithm called *"Practical Byzantine Fault Tolerance"*. This algorithm is especially used in Federated Consensus, where the participants are pre-selected, because it carries a particular weakness in the face of Sybil attacks (when one attacker can operate many nodes on the network) which would make it unsuitable for some pBFT

1.bcz.bz/2d
Interact

networks. **Find out more about the pBFT in Appendix 4 at page 236.**

Proof of Participation Consensus

Based on consideration of the various flaws and tradeoffs in the consensus mechanisms explored above, ZooBC adopts a few elements of Proof of Stake and of Federated Consensus strategies, combined with a novel algorithm developed by Blockchain Zoo to prove that a node is performing useful work for the network. We call this **"Proof of Participation"** consensus. ZooBC maintains a federation of nodes that we call the "Node Registry". Only nodes within the registry are permitted to create blocks, and their probability to create the next block is more or less equal. This is similar to Federated Consensus. However, any node operator can apply for a spot in this registry, and their admittance into the registry is governed entirely by the protocol rules, not by any centralized entity. The rate at which new nodes are added to the registry is strictly limited by the protocol, and the selection of which applicants will be added is governed by protocol rules that can be set based on the use case of ZooBC deployment. For example, it can be based on participation efforts, score gained by nodes based on a specific rule, or by mere random selection.

For ZooBC, public open blockchain to give value to the core token, we have decided to govern the selection of which nodes can stay in the registry by how much stake they are willing to lock while they are in the registry. As nodes queue to enter the node registry, priority is given to nodes with a higher locked stake. This method uses a concept of Proof of Stake, to the extent that staking tokens (a scarce resource on the network) is used as a Sybil prevention mechanism, essential for a new blockchain. **Find out more about the PoP in Appendix 4 at page 236.**

1.bcz.bz/2e
Interact

With this explanation of why a new consensus mechanism is needed, the white paper continues, in the next section, with a general description of the technology used in ZooBC.

ZooBC: a PoP Decentralized Application Platform

This section of the paper presents a reasonably complete explanation of the system in technical detail. A future discussion of security considerations and attack vectors assumes the reader's familiarity with the following mechanisms, which enables us to reason about how they combine to form the security properties of the system as a whole. This will be further developed in future versions of the white paper.

1.bcz.bz/2f
Interact

Interested in contributing to the code? Request access to the GitHub repository.

VIDEO

Watch ZooBC ALPHA Videos

Watch ZooBC Explainer Videos

FORUM

Join Discusions about ZooBC

ZOOBC Q&A

Get Your Answers on ZooBC Questions

Before We Go Any Further, a Couple of Things

First off, we have tried to make our interests clear. We want ZooBC to succeed because we believe it is the best hope for the wider adoption of blockchain. We also want to make money building things for ourselves and others on ZooBC. So to try and avoid a conflict of interest, and to promote adoption, we have made ZooBC open source, and while we will raise some funds for its further development, we don't have a direct financial interest in ZooBC. We want to get back to consulting as soon as possible. We didn't make ZooBC to get rich; we built it because we realized that blockchain, as it stands, doesn't work for lots of important use cases. We hope to make our money by making ZooBC as useful as possible, and then helping companies build their businesses atop it if they need our help.

Secondly, it goes without saying that we aren't the only people proposing a new blockchain protocol. There are dozens of them. We know that and had to think hard before adding to the confusion. We believe the only way for blockchain to be truly successful is by tackling the foundational problems of the technology, and that means building from scratch.

Accounts

The very first blockchain (Bitcoin) uses an "unspent transaction output model" of a node's current state. In this model, there is a large pool of "transaction outputs" which can be "spent" by anyone possessing the private keys corresponding to the addresses identified as the receivers of the transaction. With this model, to compute the balance of an account, a node needs to apply in sequence the first transaction through the last. While this model confers certain advantages, it is limited to modeling the ownership of titles or assets.

1.bcz.bz/2g
Interact

■ **Bitcoin Model**   ■ **ZooBC Model**

Subsequent technologies, such as Ethereum, adopted a more general "account model", where the state of the database is composed of "accounts" and their properties at any given point in time. For the same reason, in ZooBC we also use an account model to store the state of balances and other properties belonging to users in the system. With this model, the balance of an account and other properties can simply be queried from the database.

1.bcz.bz/2h
Interact

 ZOOBC Q&A

 Ask Questions about Accounts

Account Addresses

Account 1 ▾
ZBC_KM43WIKP_R2[...]47_PE5CBKBC

Most blockchain software picks a specific digital signature algorithm and requires all users to create key pairs using that algorithm. For our protocol, we take into consideration two key factors: that some signature algorithms are increasingly respected in some countries by courts of law (government-issued digital signatures and eID cards), as well as the convenience of sending funds to an account for which you are already certain the other party possesses the private key, even though it is on another blockchain.

1.bcz.bz/2j
Interact

Therefore, we design our protocol so that a user can select his own signature algorithm from a set of supported **address types.** Each type specifies a unique address type code, as well as the format of the address, and the format of the corresponding digital signature. In this way, it is possible, for example, to send funds to your friend's Bitcoin address on the ZooBC blockchain, knowing that your friend will then be able to use his Bitcoin private keys to sign valid spends of those funds on our blockchain. To be clear, this allows the use of a Bitcoin address in the ZooBC blockchain but doesn't mean that funds are transferred between the two blockchains. This will be possible with a dedicated DApp in the future versions of ZooBC.

1.bcz.bz/2k
Interact

VIDEO

What Address Types
Does ZooBC Support?

Account Properties

Each account can have a set of ***properties*** assigned to it by itself or other accounts. In some cases, the names and values of these properties may be arbitrary, while in other cases (especially in customized versions of the blockchain) certain property names may be given particular rules for how they are set and how they affect the consensus logic.

1.bcz.bz/2m
Interact

FORUM

 Join Discussions About
Account Properties

Account Types

While the most common type of account is for users, there may be other account types which share some characteristics of accounts (such as having a blockchain address, being able to have properties assigned to it, etc). but which have other characteristics which may be customized in the consensus rules.

One such account type is an **asset account,** which represents a single non-fungible asset which grants one party the right to modify its properties and allows its ownership to be transferred from account to account. It could be used, for example, for warehouse receipts, land ownership titles, etc.

1.bcz.bz/2n
Interact

Digital Twins

The digital twins core principle is that for a physical entity or an asset a digital equivalent exists in the blockchain. To replicate a physical entity – be it a machine, infrastructure, or a living being – data is extremely important. The nature of data, consisting of physical attributes, inter-object interactions, and future states, will be seamlessly exchanged between the digital and the physical worlds using blockchain. ZooBC allows users to create special account types to represent assets and be the digital part of the twins.

1.bcz.bz/2p
Interact

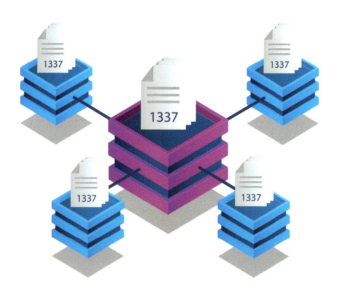

What Do We Think Is Broken With Existing Blockchain Protocols, and What ZooBC Does To Fix Those Problems?

1.bcz.bz/3n
Interact

Scan to discuss this chapter online

First off, let's explain what a protocol is. A protocol is the list of rules that govern a blockchain. A blockchain is a database, a file that lists transactions, who has what, who transacted what with whom, etc., but unlike an ordinary database it is smart enough to run itself, updating itself according to a set of rules which permit some transactions and reject others, and then replicate itself on all the computers which have agreed to run the database. Bitcoin, for example, relies on an underlying blockchain protocol called Proof of Work, which means that computers are only allowed to process those transactions if they dedicate some of their CPU power to assisting the Bitcoin network. They then get rewarded for that effort through earning bitcoins. There are lots of other protocols that use different methods. But they all need to reach the same goal: a consensus among the computers on which transactions to add, so their copies of the blockchain database all align. It's an ingenious system that promised the one thing missing from our digital, connected world -- a way to exchange something of value digitally without relying on a third party -- the government, a bank, PayPal -- organizing it and taking their cut.

But, ingenious though they are, we think that most consensus protocols only work for specific use cases and are flawed if they are applied to others. That means they are a serious brake on the development of blockchain technology.

Here's Why

First off, a blockchain is a database. And so the database is not just held by one person -- who can alter it, favor one person over another, and charge people to see the database or to register a transaction -- lots of copies of it have to be made and distributed widely enough that no one can grab them all and control them. So most blockchains require all the computers involved in the network to download and keep the full blockchain database. And, of course, over time the database becomes huge -- Bitcoin's blockchain reached, at the end of 2020, the size of 320Gb., which would take several hours, if not days or weeks, to download on a normal connection. The download is further slowed down as it is not a single request (a new node is not downloading a single file that is 320Gb in size), but, as of today, a new node must download more than 665,000 files, each representing a block, and elaborate each one with the previous in order to validate the current status of the blockchain. We think this makes blockchains inefficient and limits their usefulness, not to mention turning off people who want to get involved but don't have good enough connections or computers to download and run the blockchain software.

And this is another failing, in our view, of existing blockchains. The original idea behind the blockchain was a simple one: in order to make a decentralized network of transactions you have to somehow make it attractive for people to dedicate some of their computing and network capacity. You have to provide an incentive for them to do this. Some might do it for fun, or because they're civically minded, but you can't rely on them. They might get bored, or go on holiday, or forget to turn their computer on. In the example of Bitcoin, only those who have enough processing power needed to create new blocks, and thus validate the transactions of their choice, are rewarded with bitcoins. The rewards go to the account that arrives first in the race to solve a mathematical puzzle. In the beginning, a simple home computer was enough to participate in the race, and have a chance to win, and this guaranteed a distributed network with many nodes that were both validating blocks and creating them. But inevitably, as the network grew and the puzzles got harder, the only people able to arrive first to the race to solve the mathematical puzzle were those who had warehouses full of computers and cheap electricity.

The only people rewarded, in the Bitcoin blockchain, and the only ones deciding which transactions are included in a new block, are either groups of people who have pooled their meager computing resources together to try to win the race, or vast warehouses of computers in China with access to cheap electricity. They are the only ones earning bitcoins. The rest of the Bitcoin network, all the nodes doing the fundamental job of validating the blocks made by the few with so much computer power to always win the race, is done by people volunteering their computers, internet connection, and other related costs to the Bitcoin network. We think this, or the other methods of incentivizing users, is unfair. It discriminates against those who want to get involved but don't have the resources to do so.

But there's a bigger problem, we believe, with this protocol. And that is: it is not secure. If someone, or a group of people, controls the account that always wins the race, they can take over the decision power, de facto centralizing an otherwise decentralized system, having the power to censor what goes in the blocks and even the power to rewrite the most recent updates made to the blockchain database. This has already happened in the case of one of the most popular blockchains, Ethereum Classic, by the hands of a single attacker who after transferring funds to crypto exchanges to then withdraw bitcoin, only needed to rent online enough processing power to rewrite the most recent updates made to the Ethereum Classic blockchain, removing the transactions he previously made to transfer funds to crypto exchanges. This left the attacker with his initial funds AND the bitcoins he withdrew, at the expense of the exchanges. If the public blockchain for Ethereum Classic, protected by Proof of Work, can be attacked so easily, all the small PoW blockchains custom made for specific use cases or industries are much more vulnerable. This is one of the reasons why we wanted to create a much safer consensus system.

Transactions

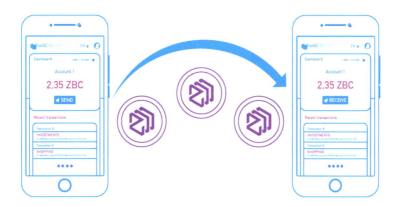

Every action executed on the ZooBC blockchain by a user is encoded in a *transaction* that specifies the action the nodes should take, the action parameters, and a data payload, and has all this digitally signed using the sender's private key. A transaction may be as simple as transferring tokens from one account to another but could have unlimited complexity, so long as its core application logic satisfies the properties that both the transaction validation and its execution are purely deterministic operations which only read from, and write to, the portion of each node's database managed by the consensus algorithm.

1.bcz.bz/2q
Interact

FORUM

Join the Discussion about Transactions

 ZOOBC Q&A

Ask Questions about Transactions

Transaction Types

We do not support, nor plan to support, general *"smart contracts"* (on-chain code), despite the popularity of this approach, because we find it unsuitable for serious decentralized business logic. Code that cannot be updated in case of bugs or changing business rules (even if by a democratic process of distributing a node software update) is a liability. Further, implementing a VM (virtual machine - an isolated virtual computer inside a computer) that supports arbitrary logic increases both the blockchain code complexity and the user complexity in terms of computing transaction execution costs and interface design.

While in future releases of ZooBC it will be possible to deploy **decentralized applications**, the first version will allow integration with centralized services on the base transaction and is deployed with a set of **transaction types** recognized by the network, where each type defines a particular behavior. While the initial set of transaction types we include is limited, our reference implementation is structured in such a way that an organization producing a customized version of this blockchain can easily add or modify the transaction logic to their node software and corresponding wallet software.

1.bcz.bz/2r
Interact

 FORUM

 Join the Discussion about Transaction Types

Transaction Propagation

When a transaction is first received from a peer or from a wallet software, the node will first confirm that the transaction is legal. This includes validating that the transaction is closed by a valid digital signature for its sending account address and that the parameters of the transaction are valid according to the transaction type's rules and the current state of the database (such as having enough balance to send funds).

If the transaction received is valid, the node will propagate the transaction by transmitting it to other connected peers, as well as store the transaction in its local mempool. In this way, valid transactions are echoed across the peer-to-peer network until they are retained in the mempool of the majority of nodes.

Upon receiving a valid transaction, each node will also return a special object we call a receipt to the sender. Receipts are used in the Proof of Participation algorithm described below.

1.bcz.bz/2s
Interact

Transaction Application

When a node receives and validates a new block (described in the section on "blocks" below), it will contain an ordered list of zero or more transactions, which the node will then apply in sequence.

For a node, applying a transaction means executing the rules associated with the transaction's type to update its local database from an old state to a new state. In the simplest example, this can mean deducting the balance from one account and adding it to another.

1.bcz.bz/2t
Interact

Multisig Transactions

Multisig accounts are accounts that require multiple signatures to post valid transactions. This is needed when at least X out of Y people need to agree for a transaction to be executed. ZooBC supports a special type of multisig account, which may specify a set of cosigners who may approve transactions from that account. An action by a multisig account is managed by the cosigners by submitting a sequence of transactions which adds to the necessary amount of signatures until enough signatures are reached for the action to be executed. The mechanics of multisig accounts and multisig transactions are described in more detail below in the Multisig section.

1.bcz.bz/2u
Interact

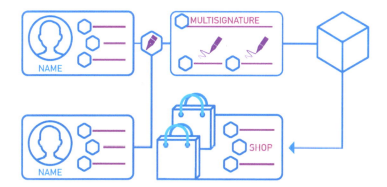

Transactions Attachments

In future versions of ZooBC, transactions will be allowed to specify large attachments to be stored in a distributed file system by the network. While the transaction itself must be propagated to all nodes, the attachment may only need to be propagated to a few nodes responsible for storing the file for others to download. More details on this are given in the section below on File Distribution.

1.bcz.bz/2v
Interact

Escrowed Transactions

When two parties must swap goods online, it is often useful to have a trusted third party keep the goods in **escrow,** such that the swap is only executed when both parties have committed their assets. Traditionally, this trusted third party holds both of the assets, and if they are not in fact so trustworthy, they may abscond with both. Therefore, it is useful to have a system in which the trusted third party may only approve or reject the transfers between parties, but in no case becomes the owner of the assets.

To facilitate this use case, ZooBC users may optionally include in the transaction the account address of an **approver**, which may either accept or reject the application of the transaction. Transactions which require approval are kept in an "escrowed" state by the blockchain, such that the funds or other assets they confer ownership of cannot be used by either the sender or the receiver until the explicit approval or rejection is completed, or the timeout returns control of the assets to the sender.

1.bcz.bz/2w
Interact

The transaction may also specify:

(A) a custom timeout: the number of blocks until, or the date /time at which, the transaction is automatically rejected (by default 1 day). The maximum timeout is 1 month;

(B) a commission: an amount of tokens which will be paid to the approver if he accepts/rejects the transaction before the timeout, by default, the cost of a transaction;

(C) instructions for the approver: in binary or a JSON format if the approver is an application on a server, or in a human language if the approver is a regular user of ZooBC;

1.bcz.bz/2x
Interact

(D) the behavior for when the transaction times out: automatically approve or reject.

In the case that the timeout is reached before the approver sends an approval or rejection, the transaction is automatically approved or rejected and the commission is returned to the sender.

In order to approve or reject an escrowed transaction, the specified approver must broadcast an **approval transaction,** referencing the hash of the pending escrowed transaction and specifying whether he approves or rejects it. While the approval transaction can be submitted automatically by centralized services, when a user needs to manually submit the approval for a transaction, the technical complexities are hidden by the wallet UI.

1.bcz.bz/2y
Interact

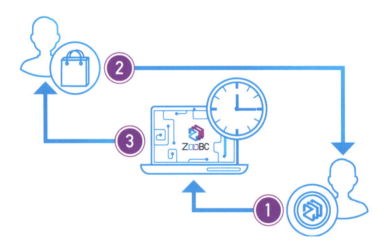

One use case of such escrow mechanism would be to configure a centralized server which manages an approver account and which is programmed to automatically approve transactions only when certain conditions have been met. For example, an escrowed transaction may specify that it should only be approved once 10 Ethereum have been transferred to a particular ETH account and set the approver to be a server which will monitor the Ethereum network to determine whether to release the funds.

Alternatively, any account may be configured to require explicit approval to accept any transaction addressed to it. In this case, if an approver account is not specified, the recipient account automatically becomes the approver. The rest of the mechanics defined above apply in exactly the same way, with the receiver of the transaction functioning as the approver.

1.bcz.bz/2z
Interact

To achieve the current normal behavior of blockchain transactions, any transaction which does not specify an approver account, and for which the receiver is not configured to require approval to accept transactions, is applied immediately upon its acceptance in a block.

The owner of an account may at any time enable or disable this mandatory approval behavior on the account by broadcasting the desired account property setting with a *required approval transaction* and specifying whether mandatory approval is enabled (default is "no").

1.bcz.bz/32
Interact

Liquid Transactions

In some cases, it may be useful to represent a continuing stream of regular payments from one account to another for the duration of a service being used. Conventional transactions are a poor fit for this purpose because they must be explicitly created and signed by a user's wallet each time. Therefore, ZooBC implements *liquid transactions.*

A liquid transaction specifies an amount of funds to be paid and the duration over which such funds should be paid. During this time, the funds will move slowly and continuously from the sender's account to the receiver's account. The sender may cancel the ongoing liquid transaction at any time, only having paid the amount that the seller has already received. And the receiver may access the funds as soon as they are received in his account by the passage of enough time. External applications may easily reference an ongoing liquid transaction to decide whether to grant a user in their system (corresponding to the sender's ZooBC account) access to features or services on their platform. This feature could also be used for payment of salaries or allowances on a continuous basis.

1.bcz.bz/33
Interact

Transaction Fees

Each transaction must include a *fee* in tokens to pay for its execution on the network. The fee for each transaction, together with new tokens generated at each new block, is distributed among the nodes in the "node registry". Requiring a fee for each transaction serves as a form of spam protection, ensuring it is costly to overwhelm the network's limited transaction volume. It also serves to incentivize block creators to include as many transactions as possible, maximizing the collective reward for producing blocks.

The *minimum fee* for a transaction is computed differently for each transaction type, then multiplied by a fee scaling constant which can be periodically adjusted. A user posting a transaction may pay more than the required minimum fee in order to be accepted in a block faster when the network load is high, but a transaction with a fee lower than the computed minimum will be rejected. For transaction A, this minimum fee can be computed:

1.bcz.bz/34
Interact

$$min\_fee(\,Tx_A\,) = type\_fee(\,TxType_A,\,Tx_A\,) * fee\_scale$$

ZOOBC Q&A

Ask Questions about Transaction Fees

So Why Should ZooBC Be Any Different?

1.bcz.bz/3s
Interact

Scan to discuss this
chapter online

Well, we have fixed these problems by re-architecting the best concepts of some existing protocols and adding some original ideas of our own. We believe the result is a stronger technology.

For example, we have changed the way people set up a new node. We reduced the work to get a new node up to date and removed the need to download the full blockchain. ZooBC uses what we call "spine blocks". They are created once a day, contain almost no data, and are cryptographically connected to the genesis block, to each other, and to the current status of the blockchain. This means that someone can set themselves up as an active node on a ZooBC blockchain by downloading a fraction of the size of an ordinary blockchain database. Now everyone with a computer and an internet connection can join and participate in the network, earning rewards.

We have also made the blockchain fairer, so that those running a ZooBC node full time get a more equitable slice of the newly created coins for their efforts. This is all part of a new consensus protocol which we call Proof of Participation, that secures the blockchain cryptographically through the activity of the nodes that are part of the network, returning to the initial idea of Satoshi Nakamoto where there is a vote for each participating computer, in other words where each participant has the same chance to with the race as any other one, no matter how much computer power they have available. Our system rewards all those running their computers or servers as nodes, based on their participation in the network. We call it Proof of Participation because ZooBC rewards nodes in the network based on the quality of their participation: essentially their uptime, the readiness of executing their part of the work when needed, and how correctly they execute their work.

And then there's the security issue. The balance with a blockchain is always between keeping things free to all comers, in line with its decentralized ethos, and keeping bad actors out (to keep things secure and protect everyone's assets). Both are flawed: completely open systems are vulnerable to the so-called Sybil Attack, where one person who can take over more than half the nodes effectively controls the whole thing, whereas at the other end a system that limits participants raises reasonable questions about whether a blockchain is really the best solution. We have taken a position somewhere in the middle, preserving the egalitarian ethos of the first system while keeping some of the discipline and security of the second, federated, system.

In our system, all people (or, better, their computers) are free to join the network, but those that want to commit full-time and earn rewards must wait in a queue to be validated and added. If they're accepted, their computer's details are filed in what we call a node registry. To avoid someone suddenly adding hundreds, or even thousands, of nodes to the node registry to become the majority and perform an attack, for security reasons only a few nodes per day are added to the node registry. The queue is ordered based on how much funds a node owner wants to lock while being part of the node registry. Nodes remain in the node registry until their 'participation score' falls below a certain level, or the node owner removes them. They are not replaced by another node, but simply the node registry becomes smaller until new nodes join.

No person is making all these decisions: it is all automated within the consensus algorithm. By ordering the queue by the amount of funds locked by the node owner (the funds are returned to them when they leave) a single user should be discouraged from hoarding nodes as part of a Sybil attack, this also incentivizes the use of the blockchain main currency in the public blockchain. For private deployment, the queue can be removed, or the score to order the queue can be based on many other factors (recorded patients at a hospital for a medical record management blockchain, clients in a hotel for a franchise management blockchain, etc).

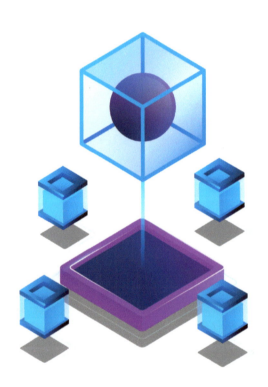

Blocks

Unlike a centralized system that receives requests from the clients in a uniquely ordered fashion (serialized), in a decentralized system such as a peer-to-peer network (where users can use any node as an entry point to post data to the network) each node may receive transactions in a different order.

WHAT IS A BLOCK?

A block is a collection of transactions that have happened during a certain amount of time and that is added to the blockchain.

BLOCK CONTENT

Index	:0
Timestamp	:17:49 1/10/2019
PreviousHash	:0000
Hash	:Dx2d05...
Data	:Block0data

A block may include valid blockchain transactions that have not entered any prior blocks. All blocks are put into a linear sequence called the blockchain. A new block includes the hash of the previous block.

BLOCK SIZE

Index	:2
Timestamp	:18:00 1/10/2019
PreviousHash	:Dxb4d3....
Hash	:Dx997g...
Data	:Block2data

Shows the file size of each block on a blockchain and therefore, how many transactions can be bundled and processed in each block. For Bitcoin, the current block size is 1MB.

BLOCK HEIGHT

Index	:1
Timestamp	:17.55 1/10/2019
PreviousHash	:Dx2d05...
Hash	:Dxb4d3...
Data	:Block1data

The total number of blocks on a given blockchain. It starts with the first block, known as the Genesis Block (height 0) and counts up from there.

BLOCK EXPLORER

A website with all transactions happening on the blockchain.

A blockchain system fundamentally solves the problem of uniquely ordering all transactions which have been broadcast to the network. Nodes are chosen in a pseudo-random lottery to append sets of transactions to the network's total transaction history. We call such a set of transactions, along with some meta-information, a block. As indicated by the name "blockchain", *blocks* are cryptographically chained together by including in the metadata of each block the hash of the previous block. Consequently, to modify the contents of any previous block would require all subsequent blocks to be re-created.

1.bcz.bz/35
Interact

 VIDEO

 Why Does ZooBC Blockchain Network Need Two Types of Blocks?

 FORUM

 Join the Discussion about Block Backups

 ZOOBC Q&A

 Ask Questions about Blocks

Structure of a Block

Each block contains several key pieces of information, which become effectively immutable as more blocks are later chained on top of it. The block contains the timestamp at which it was created, the ID number of the node which created it in the registry, a hash of all transactions included in the block, a hash of all receipts included in the block (described in the Proof of Participation section), the hash of the previous block, a special parameter used for synchronized random number generation we call the "block seed", and a few other properties.

1.bcz.bz/36
Interact

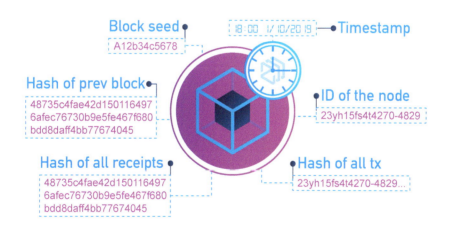

When a node receives a new block over the network, a series of validations will be performed over the block data itself, any transactions referenced by the block, and any receipts included in the block, such as ensuring that the previous block hash matches the actual last block hash the node has seen, that adequate time has passed since the timestamp of the previous block for the new block creator's position in the priority list of next creators, that the block seed is the legal value for the block creator, that the receipts included are legal according to the receipt filtering rules, and others. Only after the block passes this set of validations will it be "chained" to the last block in each node database, and the transactions included in the block will be executed in the order they are listed. The execution of the transactions will thus change each single node's database state.

1.bcz.bz/37
Interact

The Block Seed

ZooBC's Proof of Participation consensus mechanism uses many strategies that depend on pseudo-random numbers which can also be agreed upon deterministically by the network (such that each node computes the same results of its operations without explicitly sharing these results to other nodes).

Because a strong hash function produces a uniformly distributed random number from arbitrary input data, the hash of a block may be erroneously used as a source of entropy. However, as a block creator only needs to rearrange the transactions in his block, or exclude some, or change the timestamp, etc. to produce a completely new block hash, he may make many attempts to generate a hash which would be more profitable, and thus manipulate the blockchain, potentially opening the blockchain to attacks. Therefore, ZooBC includes a special property in each block called the **block seed.** This property cannot be influenced by the block creator and cannot be predicted in advance by anyone who does not have the private keys of the other block creators. The block seed is computed by the following formula:

1.bcz.bz/38
Interact

$$block\_seed_H = creator\_signatureH(\ hash(\ block\_seed_H -1\ )\ )$$

In other words, the block seed is a digital signature by the block creator on the hash of the previous block seed. By using the Ed25519 digital signature algorithm, we guarantee that the signature of a message by some particular private key has precisely one resulting signature, removing any freedom on the part of the block creator as to which block seed he is required by the protocol to include in his block.

1.bcz.bz/39
Interact

With this method, the only way a node can influence the block seed for the next block is to skip his turn (more on this in the next section) to create a block. The Proof of Participation algorithm pseudo-randomly assigns each node in the node registry a turn to create the next block, and by skipping his assigned turn, the block creator will lose participation score (if he does so repeatedly he will be ejected from the node registry).

A lower participation score immediately affects the likelihood of a node receiving coinbase rewards and dividends of transaction fees. Therefore, exercising this one degree of freedom in influencing the block seed comes at a great cost, incentivizing even maliciously inclined nodes to submit a block seed on time which may be unfavorable to them.

1.bcz.bz/3a
Interact

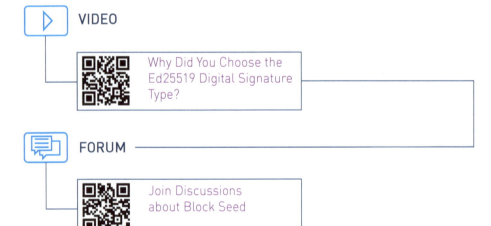

▷ VIDEO

Why Did You Choose the Ed25519 Digital Signature Type?

💬 FORUM

Join Discussions about Block Seed

Block Creator Selection

Because with the "node registry" we know the complete set of potential block creators (how a node is added to the registry is described below in the section on "node registration"), after each block, ZooBC pseudo-randomly generates a priority-ordered list of the nodes responsible for creating the next block. When a node misses its turn to create a block in this list (either because it is offline, not well connected, or deliberately skips its turn) its participation score is reduced, and the network awaits a block from the next node in the randomly ordered list.

1.bcz.bz/3b
Interact

$$order_N = hash(\ hash(BS_H) + PK_N\ )$$

Cumulative Difficulty

———

In Proof of Participation consensus, the equivalent of "highest difficulty chain" in Proof of Work consensus is the chain whose blocks have been created most reliably by one of the highest priority nodes in the list of next potential block creators, which can be called the chain with the highest **cumulative difficulty.**

To avoid attacks made by node administrators purposely leaving their nodes offline, to later rebuild a blockchain with a higher cumulative difficulty, the block creation can be done only by the first X (exact number TBD) nodes in the randomized priority list. If they are all unable to generate a block, any successive node can only produce an empty block. All the nodes before the one generating the empty block will lose participation score. Should more than one block of the same height be proposed in the network, the nodes will choose the one generated by a node with a higher place in the randomized list. If two blocks are proposed from the same creator, the one with the earlier timestamp is selected. When a node is forced to evaluate two competing chains, it will always select the chain with the highest cumulative difficulty.

1.bcz.bz/3d
Interact

The Things We've Improved

1.bcz.bz/3u
Interact

Scan to discuss this
chapter online

We believe the usefulness of a blockchain system lies in making it as compatible as possible with other blockchains, protocols, and digital systems in general. A blockchain is not a finished system in itself, but part of a broader solution. Take, for example, digital signatures. A digital signature is what it sounds like: a way for someone to sign a digital message (an email, for example) or a document (such as a PDF). For a digital signature to be trustworthy it has to be verifiable, meaning that someone who is checking the signature needs to be sure that the message or document was created by the person or entity the signature purports to belong to and that the message or document wasn't somehow changed en route. And, of course, the person who signed the document isn't able to repudiate the signature or deny that it was theirs. There are different standards of digital signature already in use by companies and governments, and so we believe it's important that blockchain technology becomes compatible with as many of these as possible. So, our third major diversion from previous blockchains is that ZooBC allows a user to choose which digital signature algorithm will secure his account and to configure an account so that it requires approval to receive transactions. By doing this, we hope to increase the blockchain's compatibility with various government regulations. For example, a ZooBC transaction could use an electronic ID card, or any other type of digital signature issued by a government, and thus recognized in court, to prove that a user agreed to receive certain funds or assets.

We also do our best to annotate and document the code. This is key to proper open sourcing, to make it as easy as possible for others to code for and on ZooBC, to make changes and improvements, to integrate ZooBC with other applications, or to develop their own application for ZooBC.

Final word

Lastly, we know our blockchain is not the solution to every problem. We know some people may prefer other solutions. We are not aiming to make ZooBC the only blockchain solution, but we are trying to expand the usefulness of blockchains beyond narrow financial use cases. ZooBC, with its Proof of Participation, creates a new standard for decentralized applications platforms where the blockchain is safe and compliant with all decentralized non-financial architectures. Our goal is to make it a technological staple, both because it's easy to learn and use and because it's flexible enough to implement a wide range of projects on it. We also hope others will join us in helping to fix the problems that are bound to arise and improve those bits that can be improved.

Multisig

When managing high-value digital assets, it is risky to have a single person holding the account key as it can be lost or compromised exposing the secured asset. Therefore, we implement native multi-signature ("multisig") features, allowing users to create accounts that require X-of-Y signatures to perform transactions. For example, out of 10 people each holding a different key, a transaction can be performed by just 4 of those 10 signing it.

1.bcz.bz/3e
Interact

 VIDEO

 Explaining Multisig Mechanism

FORUM

 Join Discussions about Multisig

 ZOOBC Q&A

 Get Your Questions about Multisig Answered

Multisig Addresses

One of the address types we support is a ***multisig address,*** being the hash of a set of details regarding who is allowed to sign on behalf of the address. We refer to this set of raw details as a ***multisig info.***

This design leaves open the possibility that, until the time of signing, the set of addresses that control a multisig address doesn't need to be revealed.

1.bcz.bz/3f
Interact

Multisig Info Object

Field	Description
MinSigs	The minimum number of signatures out of the provided address list which must be present to execute a transaction from this multisig address.
Nonce ("Access Code")	A free number field allowing unique multisig addresses to be created between the same set of addresses.
Addresses	An alphabetically-ordered list of account addresses that may legally sign for this multisig address. These addresses can, in turn, be multisig addresses, allowing for hierarchical multisig.

The Multisig Transaction Type

ZooBC implements all aspects of multisig behavior through a single transaction type. The behavior of this transaction type is somewhat complex because it implements both on-chain and off-chain multisig behavior with the possibility to preserve the anonymity of the signers and conceal the transaction being signed until the moment that all needed pieces of information have been exposed to the blockchain.

The transaction body of a multisig transaction has 3 optional components: a multisig info object (described above) revealing which set of addresses may sign for the transaction, the transaction being signed on (either the unsigned full data of the transaction or its transaction hash), and a list of signatures on the transaction hash by other signers.

1.bcz.bz/3g
Interact

To manage the multisig process, the node keeps three consensus-managed tables: the multisig info table, the pending transaction table, and the pending signatures table. When a multisig info object is included in a multisig transaction, it will be saved in the multisig info table along with its hash (which is the corresponding multisig address.) When an unsigned transaction is included with a multisig transaction, the unsigned transaction and its hash are recorded in the pending transactions table. When some signatures on a transaction hash are included in a multisig transaction, a record for each is accumulated in the pending signatures table.

1.bcz.bz/3h
Interact

In this way a multisig transaction gets executed as soon as all the necessary parts (the transaction itself, the list of co-signers, and the needed signatures) are added to the blockchain by being included into validated blocks, independently of the order they have received. After adding any transaction with multisig-related data to the relevant tables, each node will evaluate whether enough information is available to execute the specified pending transaction.

Specifically: if, for the specified pending transaction, the sender address is known to be a multisig address (because a multisig info object hashing to that address has already been revealed), there are enough signatures on its transaction hash in the pending signatures table (where each signature must be from an address specified in the multisig info), and the transaction is still valid at the time of application, then the pending transaction is executed as if it was a normal transaction on the blockchain occurring in place of the multisig transaction.

All three types of data have an expiry time, therefore the multisig transaction will only execute in the case that these conditions are met in a timely fashion. Afterward, unused pieces of data will be pruned from the consensus-managed local tables of each node.

1.bcz.bz/3k
Interact

Multisig Use Cases

The purpose of the complexity of this transaction type is to give users the power through one tool to accomplish various flavors of multisig transaction behavior. For clarity, some of the use cases which may be satisfied by this design are described below.

Off-Chain Multisig

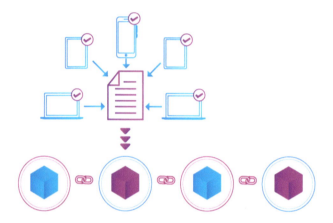

In this case, the behavior of the multisig transaction approximates the classical multisig behavior of Bitcoin and other blockchains, where the account controllers work together off-chain to prepare a single valid transaction that will be immediately evaluated and applied once broadcast to the network.

In the simplest case, all optional parameters of a multisig transaction may be supplied in one transaction, including the multisig info describing who may sign for the account, the transaction details to be executed by the account, and all needed signatures from the other account controllers.

1.bcz.bz/3p
Interact

On-Chain Multisig

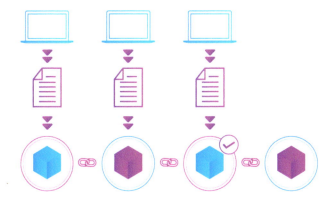

This may be useful in cases where some participants wish to prove their existing signatures on-chain before others feel confident about providing their own signatures, or in cases when another required signer cannot be contacted off-chain by the other co-signers but may be alerted by some third-party application that a multisig transaction awaits his signature.

If the multisig info and pending transaction are already revealed, other account controllers may submit their signatures for the transaction as separate multisig transactions. In the extreme case, each needed signer may submit a multisig transaction appending only his own signature to the pending transaction hash, which will simply be accumulated in the pending signatures table until the number of signatures needed to execute the pending transaction is reached.

1.bcz.bz/3q
Interact

Anonymizing Multisig Addresses

This behavior may be useful in cases where it is desirable to not reveal the controllers of an asset until they must act, especially if they are in conditions where they must individually submit their signatures on-chain. Alternately, this may be used as a mechanism intended to discourage someone from posting a transaction unless they really mean it: a pending transaction may be irrevocably committed (signed and ready to execute), giving anyone who possesses the multisig info the power to single-handedly force the transaction to be executed by revealing it.

Due to the structure of the multisig transaction, it is acceptable to submit a pending transaction from a multisig address, and all needed signatures on that transaction, before the multisig info (such as which addresses may sign for the transaction) are revealed. To further create plausible deniability for the actual multisig participants, many other accounts may blindly submit signatures for the given transaction hash, even if they are not co-signers of the multisig account. In this case, the pending transaction will be executed as soon as a multisig info matching its sender address is submitted in a separate multisig transaction.

1.bcz.bz/3r
Interact

▷ VIDEO

Multisig and Key
Management

Concealing Pending Transactions

This behavior may be useful when it is not convenient for the controllers of an account to pass around a partially-signed transaction, yet they do not want to reveal what action they plan to take unless it collects the necessary support of other account controllers (for example, a board of directors voting to fire the CEO, who can herself access and see the blockchain). Like above, this may also be used as a privacy protection mechanism, where a pending transaction will be executed the moment any person who possesses it chooses to submit it.

Even if the multisig info is already revealed, the unsigned pending transaction itself may be hidden from the blockchain until enough signers have already submitted their signatures on its hash (in order to produce the correct signature, they must be given the contents of this transaction off-chain.) In this case, the pending transaction will be executed as soon as its full data is submitted in a separate multisig transaction.

1.bcz.bz/3t
Interact

Hierarchical Multisig

This behavior may be useful when complex organizational structures are responsible for an asset. Say, for example, approval for a transaction is needed from 2 out of 3 departments, where each department, in turn, requires the approval of 3 out of 5 managers, and where perhaps a few of the managers represent oversight committees, which themselves must cast a majority vote to approve.

Because a pending transaction may be any valid transaction on the blockchain, it may also itself be a multisig transaction. In this way, the creator of a multisig address may specify another multisig address as one of the controlling accounts. There is no limitation on how many multisig layers may be created this way.

In this case, a pending transaction may be created from the top-level multisig address. Before this transaction may be executed, a signature must be added by the controlling multisig address. The multisig transaction to add this signature becomes, itself, a pending transaction which must satisfy the conditions specified by its own multisig info before it will be executed.

1.bcz.bz/3w
Interact

A New Type of Blockchain, in a Sea of Blockchains

1.bcz.bz/3v
Interact

Scan to discuss this
chapter online

Creating a new platform such as ZooBC in a fast-growing technological industry, such as the blockchain one, is difficult enough. Doing so without the millions of dollars usually raised with funding rounds like ICOs or ITOs further added to the challenge. In addition, we were trying to create a use case for ZooBC using our very own consensus mechanism: PoP, aka Proof of Participation.

Where did this all lead to?

Towards a challenging, yet aspirational goal, where two technological visionaries (Roberto Capodieci and Barton Johnston) met with their friend and technical whiz, Stefano Griggio, and other industry leaders, to make their ZooBC dream a reality, as part of their newly founded company, Blockchain Zoo. But before that was to happen, they needed to ensure that their vision stood the test of time.

It was very important from the beginning that ZooBC actually fixed problems that other blockchains couldn't fix, couldn't fix well, or didn't address at all. Making a new platform open-sourced, without investor funding, and without wanting to copy another blockchain's code, ideas, and implementations, was tricky.

Forging ahead, despite the obstacles.

For this project to be viable, it needed several factors to work. A novel approach. An implementation of that approach into a working product. A great team of developers to build said product, as well as a marketing department to bring awareness to the public. An ecosystem of services (e.g. blockchain consulting, public workshops, and online education). Plus an inspiring space, where all of these ideas could thrive. Eventually, the team was built on the island of Bali, in the Blockchain Zoo offices.

ZooBC, like Bali, often went through a number of super-rainy days. And like the tropical island, there were times of turbulence, where hitting a wall with the development of the blockchain's consensus system, or a lack of funds, felt like the end of days for the nascent company of Blockchain Zoo and the ZooBC project.

Finding hope, as the journey began.

It's true that hope was almost lost so many times, but the team persevered. This was because the original concepts for the ZooBC blockchain were interesting, powerful, and had the potential to revolutionize, as well as expand, blockchain's bright future.

By seeking to democratize network nodes thanks to their novel Proof of Participation consensus model, reward these nodes (active computers) by scoring their P2P activity their participation in the network, and make the system more secure against Sybil attacks, the team would then be inspired to keep going against the odds and build a thriving new business — built around a dream.

The next stage of this book describes the beginnings of ZooBC as more than just an idea between three blockchain and tech enthusiasts, their many hurdles, and the start of the Blockchain Zoo dream.

Fee Scaling (Governance)

One difficulty with transaction fees on any public and permissionless blockchain network arises from extreme volatility in the value of the underlying token. Ideally, the cost of fees to process transactions will remain approximately constant with respect to the stable currencies which users exchange for the token. For example, if the average minimum transaction fee is 1 token, this will fail to reduce network spam or incentivize block creators when the token value is US$0.0001, but it will likely make all transactions prohibitively expensive if the token value reaches US$100.

1.bcz.bz/3x
Interact

There are many strategies to approach this issue. At one extreme, the fee could be set by a trusted third party which signs such new information against a public key agreed upon by the entire blockchain, but such centralization is anathema to the ethos of decentralized systems, as it can be manipulated by a single actor who is beyond accountability. At the other extreme, nodes could attempt to draw independently from public sources, such as exchanges, the value of the token in a stable currency, in order to change the transaction fee amount to match a fixed value in stable currency; yet, because such data is not tracked by the blockchain's own consensus, this could lead to forks when such external information is not consistent when queried by different nodes at different times.

Therefore, we conclude that safely reaching consensus on data from outside of the blockchain, such as the token's value against other currencies, cannot be accomplished automatically. We implement a system by which operators of registered nodes on the network may take a regular vote on the appropriate multiplier, which we call the fee scale, for minimum transaction fees. This allows the transaction fee amount to keep the same value against a stable currency, even if the blockchain's main token value fluctuates.

1.bcz.bz/3z
Interact

It is potentially dangerous to put such a critical network parameter in the hands of node operators. A more complete discussion of the risk will be presented in future work. However, we prefer this risk over the inherent risk of imposing a static minimum fee for the reasons described above.

1.bcz.bz/42
Interact

We also prefer this risk because we believe it can be mitigated by balancing two competing incentives of node operators which should constrain each other. On the small scale, a node operator wishes to maximize the transaction fees he collects in each block by pushing the network fee scale higher. But on the large scale, network fees that are high will reduce user's willingness to pay for any transactions on the blockchain, and this lack of usability may be reflected in the token price, which determines the real value a node operator stands to gain, incentivizing him to push the network fee scale lower.

1.bcz.bz/43
Interact

The vote-based adjustment of the fee scale is accomplished via three mechanisms: node operators committing to their votes, node operators revealing the votes they have previously committed, and the averaging calculation used to compute the new network fee scale.

1.bcz.bz/44
Interact

 ZOOBC Q&A

 Get Your Questions about
Fee Scaling Answered

Committing to Fee Votes

First, the node operator needs to cast their vote on how much, if any, the fee scale should be adjusted. The fee is adjusted every month. Each of these one-month periods is further divided into two phases: a **commitment phase,** when the votes are cast, and a reveal phase, when the votes are revealed and counted. During the commitment phase, owners of nodes in the registry may submit a **commit fee vote** transaction.

1.bcz.bz/45
Interact

First, the node operator's wallet will create a **fee vote** object. This object contains a recent block hash, the corresponding block height, the user's vote on what the new network fee scale should be, and the account's digital signature on the above information. Because we intend for node operators to vote in a way that stabilizes transaction fees against major fiat currencies, the wallet will collect this information from exchanges, calculate an appropriate value by which to multiply the fee, and strongly recommend the value of the vote to the user. However, there is no way for the blockchain to validate this value, therefore it is only a recommendation, and the user may enter any value they wish.

The extra pieces of information in the fee vote object (block hash, account's signature) are included to make the hash of the fee vote object resilient to attacks where an attacker may simply guess what fee scale the user is voting for, hash their guess, and confirm their guess by comparing it to the vote commitment hash.

As recent block hashes will be different for each voting period, and a digital signature is performed on these properties, anyone not possessing the account's private key is unable to reproduce the object and is therefore not able to reproduce the resulting hash of the object and determine by a guess-and-check method the vote being committed by a user.

Once the fee vote object is prepared, its hash is computed and included in the commit fee vote transaction, which is then signed and submitted to the network by the user. When this transaction is included in a block and applied, a record will be kept in the node's database indicating the commitment hash. Such transactions may only successfully be included in blocks during the commitment phase of the voting period.

1.bcz.bz/49
Interact

Revealing Fee Votes

After the commitment phase of the voting period has concluded, the reveal phase begins. This is when the votes are recorded on the blockchain and accumulated. During this phase it is OK for the owners of registered nodes to submit a **reveal fee vote** transaction.

1.bcz.bz/4a
Interact

The reveal fee vote transaction includes the full contents of the fee vote object which the user previously committed to. It is then signed and submitted to the network. In order to be accepted by nodes as a valid transaction, the hash of the submitted fee vote object must match the commitment hash already submitted in the commitment phase by the user.

Additionally it must be verified that the "recent block hash" parameter is within the time frame of this voting period and that the digital signature on the parameters is a valid signature for the node operator's account. When the transaction is successful, the user's vote is recorded in the blockchain. Values for new votes are accumulated during the reveal phase.

1.bcz.bz/4c
Interact

Adjusting the Network Fee Scale

The end of the reveal phase marks the end of the entire voting period, which immediately begins the next voting period by initiating another commitment phase. On the first block of the new voting period, a calculation is performed of all the successfully revealed votes from the previous voting period to determine the new value of the network fee scale parameter.

The collected votes for the new value are ordered from least to greatest, and the number in the middle of the ordered list is selected as the new value (the median value). We use this approach, rather than averaging the votes, to avoid giving a small number of outliers the power to significantly bias the outcome. In the case that most votes are clustered together, even if a minority voted much higher or lower, we select the middle of the cluster as the most accurate representation of the majority opinion.

1.bcz.bz/4e
Interact

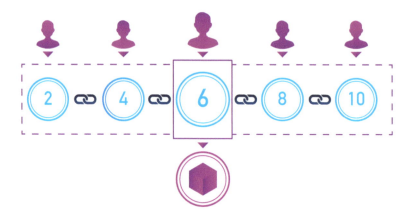

After this value is selected, it is further constrained such that it may only increase to a maximum of twice the previous value, or decrease to half the previous value. This reduces swings in the fee and creates a degree of predictability and stability for users.

1.bcz.bz/4f
Interact

This new network fee scale value is applied going into the new voting period. During this time, users can expect the parameter value to be constant, and wallets can query the nodes for the current value of the parameter in order to automatically recommend a permitted minimum transaction fee.

1.bcz.bz/4g
Interact

Depending on experiments, we may also allow a grace period for transactions created during the previous fee scale period to still be valid. We wish to avoid a condition where congested transactions in the mempool, which included a fee that was legal at the time they were submitted, are suddenly excluded as the result of a change in the minimum fee parameter.

1.bcz.bz/4h
Interact

Note on General Governance

While the description of voting mechanism in the above sections are specific to managing the "network fee scale" parameter, they could easily be applied to any other network parameter deemed safe to be placed in the hands of the majority owners of the node registry. These could include the maximum number of transactions per block, the average time between blocks, the rate at which new nodes are admitted into the node registry, or others.

Depending on the success of this limited form of governance mechanism in the first version of the ZooBC blockchain, we may apply this strategy to other constant parameters in future versions. This is consistent with our gradual and conservative approach to extending ZooBC through an iterative process of analysis, design, and deployment. A list of constants that ZooBC needs to operate is at the end of this paper.

1.bcz.bz/4j
Interact

Thailand, Baby!

1.bcz.bz/3y
Interact

Scan to discuss this
chapter online

Sometimes, having fun, relaxing, and having casual brainstorms is the best way to move forward.

A few months into our new blockchain project, we had gotten to the point of realizing that the Proof of Participation mechanism was a realistic goal. In understanding all the aspects of what would be needed from us, we also realized we needed help. We called our friend and business partner, Stefano Griggio, to see if he was interested in joining us on this venture. He was definitely in, and the three of us decided to go grab some much-needed respite for a week in Thailand!

We had planned for the trip to consist mainly of relaxation, brainstorming, and time spent in a creative space. We wanted uninterrupted time to get to the technical aspects of building a new blockchain, and we knew Stefano was better technically than even we were. We spent time researching and experimenting to make sure that what we had was not only novel but that it was an idea worth implementing.

We spent time looking at other blockchains that we liked and their unique components. We took the concepts that we liked and that worked for us, and either changed or left the others. From there, we sat and discussed what we'd each like to see in a new blockchain that simply didn't exist yet.

One of the ideas we tossed around was creating a new and improved version of NXT. Yet as the day went on, we kept talking about adding or subtracting features, while shifting things around within the existing NXT formatting. That was when we realized we had essentially used NXT as a starting point and had then created a unique blockchain instead. We took some inspiration from other blockchain platforms too, of course.

With Proof of Participation we wanted the different types of work nodes to be measured and rewarded accordingly. People around the world get paid for doing different jobs, as well as the varying demands of those jobs. Why should nodes in a blockchain be any different?

We realized we wanted to focus on creating something solid, practical, and feasible, which allowed us to deliver ZooBC in a relatively short time. We were giving ourselves two years to get this done, and at the end of this week, we had only a couple of documents in our hands with some ideas, some concepts, and a lot of hope.

Node Registration

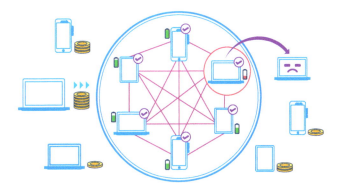

Although anyone can run a node and connect to the network, we restrict the creation of blocks and the distribution of coinbase rewards to a subset of registered nodes. The process of how new nodes can become registered, and how nodes are ejected from the registry, is managed entirely by the network protocol. This means that no single user or account has the authority to promote a node or change its status; nodes only change status by the automatic application of the protocol rules. This design has three key motivations:

1.bcz.bz/4k
Interact

- To prevent theft of private keys;
- To prevent an attacker from taking over a majority of nodes;
- To allow for the removal of unproductive nodes or those using a novel, unexpected, method to abuse the network.

Following is a more detailed explanation of the purpose and mechanism for each aspect of the above. First, we separate the private key of the node owner's ZooBC account from the process of block creation. In blockchains where blocks are secured via digital signatures rather than a direct Proof of Work, the private key of the account of the user managing the node (the account that receives the coinbase rewards) must be present directly on the node, which is an online computer used to create blocks.

This creates a security hazard where the account's private key may be hacked, or intercepted, by an attacker. If the computer hosting the node is breached or a man in the middle (MITM) attack is executed. For hosted nodes running in virtual private servers (VPS), it could be as simple as the operator of the data center accessing the VPS file system and reading the private keys, giving them access to the account with funds.

1.bcz.bz/4m
Interact

Second, we regulate the rate at which nodes can join the family of block creators in the node registry. To prevent attacks on the Proof of Participation algorithm, where an attacker can register many nodes' public keys at the same time (thereby flooding the node registry and controlling a large majority of nodes capable of creating new blocks), the protocol rules only allow a limited number of new and active nodes to join the node registry during each set period. Restricting the registration of new nodes *en messe* preempts this attack.

1.bcz.bz/4n
Interact

Third, we can remove nodes that are offline (or simply don't participate in the network) from the node registry. The Proof of Participation algorithm described below has a scoring system that punishes nodes that don't participate. Any nodes which fall to zero participation score are automatically removed from the registry; if they later become active they are automatically added to the queue to re-join the node registry.

1.bcz.bz/4p
Interact

Beyond these motivations, it is also used as a weighting coefficient on a node's likeliness to collect coinbase rewards. This incentivizes nodes to remain online and participating. How this score is calculated is described in detail in the later section on Proof of Participation.

By maintaining a federation of nodes which continuously prove their active participation on the network, we create a foundation for the application platform we will deliver with the next version of ZooBC. Using the blockchain to reach consensus on the state of the registry will allow DApps to leverage faster federated consensus algorithms between registered nodes in future versions.

1.bcz.bz/4q
Interact

Although the node registry is not leveraged in its full capacity for this first version of the ZooBC technology, we intend this first deployment to gather information about its safety, the ease and intuitiveness of its management by node operators, and how it can be abused, in order to address any major issues before continuing to develop new strategies on top of it.

VIDEO

 Fixing Critical Bugs of Node Registration

 How Node Registration and Participation in ZooBC Work

What Do You Need to Run the ZooBC Node?

How Can Users Register Their Nodes to the Wallet?

 What Tips Could You Give to People Who Intend to Run the ZooBC Nodes?

 What to Keep in Mind When Running the ZooBC Node

Why Do Nodes Need to Register Themselves on the ZooBC Block-chain Network Before Finding Blocks?

What Can a Node Runner Do to Make Sure He Always Stays in the Node Registry and Gains Rewards?

 FORUM

 Join Discussions about Network

 Join Discussions about Node Registration

 ZOOBC Q&A

Get your Questions about Registration Answered

Get your Questions about Nodes Answered

The Node Registry Life Cycle

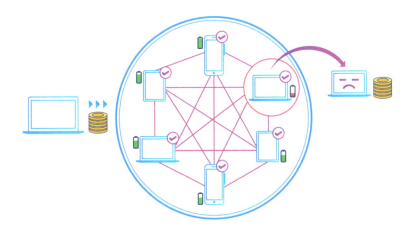

Once a user has installed a node and allowed it to synchronize with the network, she may apply for a spot in the node registry by submitting a register node transaction. This transaction includes some details about the node, as well as a proof that the owner controls the node's private key. Upon submission of this valid registration request, the node enters into the registration queue. The creation of newly available seats in the registry, and the replacement of nodes in the registry by those in the queue, are strictly regulated by the protocol rules. When seats become available, new nodes are admitted into the registry from the registration queue.

1.bcz.bz/4r
Interact

When a node is first in line in the registration queue, the protocol first requires it to prove its participation in the network for a brief period before admitting it to join the registry and begin creating blocks. If a node remains in the queue for more than 30 days without participating, its locked funds are returned to the node's owners account, and the node is removed from the queue. This means that if the node owner wants to add her node to the queue again, she needs to submit a register node transaction and pay the corresponding fee.

1.bcz.bz/4s
Interact

Once a node has been admitted into the registry, it becomes subject to the Proof of Participation algorithm, which will gradually modify the node's participation score upwards or downwards based on its behavior on the network. The registry seat also entitles the owner to participation rewards (coinbase), with the amount of rewards received being proportional to the node's participation score.

During the node's tenure in the registry, the node's owner may update her its details as she sees fit by submitting an **update node transaction.** For example, the node owner may need to change the node's key pair, or she may decides to increase her locked balance to increase her chances of remaining in the registry.

Additionally, if the node's owner loses her account's private key, so long as she still controls the node's private key, she may submit a *claim node transaction* from her new account to recover her locked funds, although this will remove the node from the registry.

This has the deliberate consequence that if an attacker can access your node's private key, he can effectively claim any funds you had locked to register the node. This forces node owners to take care of the security of their nodes, while making a node useless if hacked. The significance of this risk to the security of the Proof of Participation algorithm is discussed in more detail below.

1.bcz.bz/4w
Interact

A user may wish to remove their node from the registry deliberately to reclaim their locked funds, in which case they can submit a **remove node transaction.** This will credit any locked funds for the node back to the owner's account, and the node score is lost. There is no way to reclaim the locked funds of the node without simultaneously removing it from the node registry.

Finally, a node may be automatically ejected from the registry if its participation score drops to zero. In this case, the funds locked with the node registration are still left with the node, which automatically joins the queue to re-enter the node registry, sparing a node owner in good faith from having to pay the fee to add the node to the queue again. As described above, as long as this node remains offline, it will repeatedly fail the trial period before it can be added to the registry again until it is removed from the queue.

1.bcz.bz/4y
Interact

Some aspects of this general process are discussed below in more detail.

The Node Registry

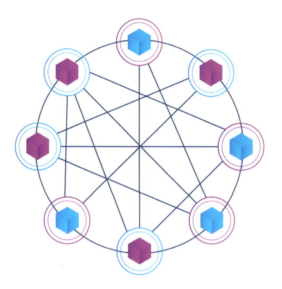

Each node on the network maintains a table we call the node registry. The registry serves first and foremost as a mapping between user account addresses and the nodes they operate, empowering the nodes to sign blocks on the user's behalf without exposing their private keys, and allowing the user's account to be directly rewarded for the node's participation.

1.bcz.bz/4z
Interact

Each node's entry in the registry declares the following properties:

Field	Description
Public Key	The public key corresponds to the node's configured private key. When blocks or Proof of Participation messages are produced by a node, the signatures can be validated against this key.
Account Address	The account address of the node owner's account. This account may legally change or remove the node registration, and any participation rewards earned by the node are credited to this account.
Locked Balance	An amount of funds that the node's owner has put up as collateral to compete for a spot in the registry, and to incentivize her to maintain the security of her node's private key.
Participation Score	A score tracked for this node over time by the Proof of Participation algorithm. A higher score increases the number of rewards received, while falling to zero will cause the node to be ejected from the registry.

The Node's Public Key

Each node keeps its own private key, which is used to sign blocks on its owner's behalf. The corresponding public key is published to the network through the process described below, allowing other nodes to validate that blocks and peer-to-peer messages that originated from this node are authentic.

In the simplest case, the node's private key is kept on the node's hard drive in a configuration file, however for node operators who are more security conscious, Blockchain Zoo is working to allow a separate hardware device to sign on behalf of the node. This is to mitigate the following vulnerability:

If a node's private key is compromised, the attacker may be able to impersonate this node on the network to others. However, as described in the Claim Node section below, the attacker will also be able to claim the node operator's locked funds and kick the node from the registry.

In the event that a user learns his node's private key may have been compromised, he can rotate the node's key pair and update his entry in the node registry at any time, by signing an update node transaction with his account's private key.

1.bcz.bz/54
Interact

Locked Balance

To maintain a node in the registry, the owner's account must lock some amount of ZooBC tokens. When a node is added to the registration queue, this amount is deducted from the owner's account and kept in trust by the network. Later, if the node is ejected from the registry queue, or if the owner removes it from the registry or the queue deliberately, the locked funds are returned entirely to the owner's account.

Locked funds are used to prioritize the addition of nodes to the registry. New spots in the registry are only opened gradually, and the "size of a node's locked balance is used to prioritize which node in the queue will take the next available spot. In this way, although ZooBC doesn't use a variation of Proof of Stake consensus, a user's funds on the network are still relevant to his ability to be admitted into the node registry in a timely fashion. In this first version of the ZooBC technology, we still require this fund locking as a mechanism to prevent Sybil attacks, as funds on the network are a scarce resource, and keeping them locked ensures that they cannot be used twice by the same actor.

However, we have confined the significance of a user's balance to this particular corner of the protocol; in future versions of the technology we will apply an alternate Sybil prevention mechanism unrelated to the user's account balance. We will substitute that without otherwise modifying the mechanics of the system. Doing so will fulfill a major long-term design goal of the ZooBC project: management, on a trustless network, of assets that have a value greater than the market cap of the native cryptocurrency of the blockchain, or even running a blockchain without native currency while at the same time guaranteeing its trustworthiness and security.

1.bcz.bz/57
Interact

The Registration Queue

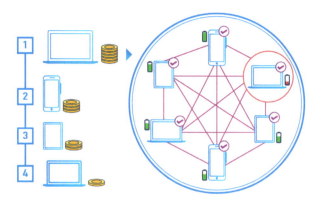

The registration queue is a list of nodes which have been identified by a node registration transaction, and whose owner has committed an amount of locked funds, but which have not yet been admitted into the node registry.

The queue is prioritized by the amount of funds locked by each registering account, such that the account which committed the most funds in its registration transaction will be the first in line to be added to the registry when new admissions are allowed.

New admissions are taken from the queue into the registry at a regular interval. The rate at which new nodes are accepted is a function of the existing size of the node registry, such that when the registry is small, new nodes will be added slowly, but as the registry grows new nodes will be admitted faster. This rate is fundamentally a security requirement of the Proof of Participation algorithm, as an attacker could trick the algorithm if he were suddenly able to take control of a major fraction of the registry. Admitting nodes gradually gives the algorithm enough time to remove cheating nodes before they can accumulate a majority (see Node Registration, above).

1.bcz.bz/59
Interact

Registering a Node

Before registering her node, the owner must collect a special message from it called a ***proof of ownership.*** This message simply contains the owner's account address, a recent block hash, and the height of the block hash. The message is signed off by the node's private key.

The proof of ownership message is then bundled inside a register node transaction, together with the node's public key, the amount of funds to lock from the sending account, the account's signature, and the fee for the transaction. To prevent malicious users from abusing the register node transaction, the fee to add a node to a queue is much higher than most transaction types.

When this transaction is executed by the network, the balance specified by the owner will be locked, and the node will be added to the registration queue. The locked funds are taken from the user's account and held in trust by the network, until such time as the node exits the queue or registry for any reason, at which time the funds are returned to the user's account in full with a 1-day delay.

The wallet application we provide helps to smooth the process of collecting the proof of ownership message from the user's node and assembling the transaction for the network, ensuring the user has an intuitive interface and needs no specialized technical knowledge of the system to perform this operation.

1.bcz.bz/5d
Interact

Claiming a Node

By design, it is not particularly dangerous if a user loses control of a node's private key, since it is only used to create blocks and to prove a node's identity in the Proof of Participation algorithm. As described above, this isolation is a key motivation for separating the node's private key from an account's private key.

However, there is a type of "key sharing" attack on the Proof of Participation algorithm where all nodes may voluntarily share their private keys with each other. If all users agreed to share their node keys, they would undermine the central assumption the algorithm is premised on: namely that only a user's node may generate a valid digital signature, proving the node was online and participating with the network at the time.

Therefore, in the case that a user comes into possession of another node's private key, ZooBC allows this user to "claim" the node's locked funds, which will also eject that node from the registry. Such a "key sharing" attack then requires enormous trust in the other participants in the scheme not to steal funds from each other, while still allowing a user to limit the damage that can be done to them by only locking in their node an amount of funds they are willing to put at risk. This incentivizes node operators to take seriously the security of their nodes, as nodes are custodians of the private keys that control such locked funds.

1.bcz.bz/5f
Interact

Ejection from the Node Registry

If at any time the participation score of a node in the registry drops to zero, the network's consensus rules dictate that the node will automatically be returned from the registry into the queue. In this way, a node must be consistently online and participating to remain in the registry and collect coinbase rewards. Ejection from the queue does not penalize the user's locked funds, which are returned in full to the node owner's account.

1.bcz.bz/5g
Interact

Building Blocks

At the dawn of ZooBC, before it was a new blockchain project, we were using a lot of Proof of Stake and Proof of Work platforms with our clients. In doing so, we understood how many pain points came with each mechanism. We found ourselves working day and night to ensure the total security of those systems and finally realized there was no way to make either system 100% secure. We knew we needed something different, and that what we needed didn't exist, yet.

That was probably the moment that ZooBC and the Proof of Participation mechanism were born.

When you think of brainstorming an idea, you probably consider options like mind maps, long lists, or even just an afternoon spent chatting with friends about that topic. When ZooBC was in its early conceptual stages, there was certainly a lot of that. Yet brainstorming blockchain ideas comes with an added element: there are problems that need immediate solutions. New problems.

As we sat around throwing ideas out about how to make the Proof of Participation consensus mechanism work, one of us would discuss a possibility, and then oftentimes the other would immediately find massive problems with it. This back and forth went on until we were able to finally pin down the consensus mechanism we have eventually created.

Once we had the general idea and a plan in mind, we began our first conceptual tests. Our first tests were informative, to say the least, but our initial ideas didn't stick. At first we had a series of nodes set up where one node sat in judgment of the others, trying to ensure that all participating nodes were staying honest.

To cut a long story short, there was no real way to prove they were being honest. Even if we could find a way to tell empirically whether the nodes were being honest or not, there was no way to ensure that they had a reason to be honest and reliable.

Proof of Participation

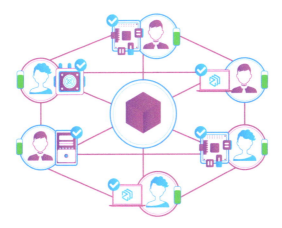

We propose a novel consensus algorithm that involves proving that registered nodes are reliably online and propagating data to each other, computing a participation score for each, and using this score as a weighting coefficient to the node's pseudo-random chance to be elected to receive coinbase rewards. If a registered node's participation score falls to zero it is automatically ejected from the node registry.

1.bcz.bz/5h
Interact

Our intentions with this strategy include promoting the availability of network nodes, more evenly distributing stewardship of the blockchain history among many parties, and more evenly rewarding the participation of all nodes composing the network. Additionally, we create an incentive scheme for the network of all registered nodes to organize itself into an optimal topology thus minimizing the number of hops any piece of data must take to propagate through the entire network.

1.bcz.bz/5j
Interact

VIDEO

 What Is
Proof of Participation
in Simple Words?

 How Does the
Proof of Participation
Algorithm Work?

Proof of Participation
vs. Other Consensus
Algorithms

Why Does ZooBC
Blockchain Use a
Proof of Participation
Algorithm?

 FORUM

 Join Discussions
about Core General

 Join Discussions about
Proof of Participation

 Join Discussions
about Consensus

 ZOOBC Q&A

 Get Your Questions
about Participation
Answered

 Get Your
Questions about
Proof of Participation
Answered

Overview

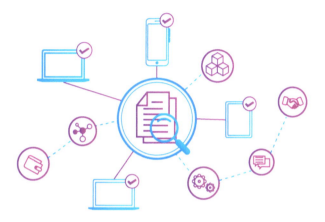

"Participation" could be defined in many ways, but for the purposes of this algorithm we mean that a node is transmitting pieces of blockchain-related data (such as blocks and transactions) to many other nodes in a timely fashion. While tracking the entire set of node-to-node transmissions is infeasible, we use a random sampling strategy to pick some small subset of transmissions from the network to evaluate who is participating.

Such proofs of transmission would be meaningless if they could be produced on demand; therefore, nodes must regularly publish "commitments" of their transmission activity to the network. When a node is called on to produce some small sample of its past transmission activity, it should also prove that the records it produces were included in commitments already published on the blockchain, which makes such records impossible to produce just-in-time.

1.bcz.bz/5m
Interact

The ZooBC network protocol specifies that each transmission should return a **receipt:** a special object, digitally signed by the receiver, which uniquely identifies the sender. The receipt is a claim that a particular piece of data was transmitted between those nodes at that time. A receipt object also includes a **commitment:** the Merkle root of a set of other receipts which had previously been collected by the receiver.

1.bcz.bz/5n
Interact

When a node creates a block, it can include some receipts of its past transmission activity. These receipts can be validated objectively by all nodes using several criteria. The number and quality of the included receipts are used to calculate whether the node's participation score should rise or fall.

1.bcz.bz/5p
Interact

As we wish to measure only recent activity on the network, we impose a **height filter** on receipts which may be included in a block, such that receipts expire some number of blocks after they were created. The expiration time is a function of the number of registered nodes, because a greater number of block creators means a greater average time between blocks created by any given node, which consequently expands the average time we expect between a receipt's publication and the time it was previously committed.

1.bcz.bz/5q
Interact

Wishing to prove the node has received and propagated the full set of data items on the blockchain, we impose a **data filter** on the receipts which may be included in a block. Based on the number of data items recently included in the blockchain, we pseudo-randomly restrict the set of data hashes which may be legally included, in a way that is not predictable before the block creator's turn. This ensures that a node must keep receipts from all data items transmitted in order to reliably produce the randomly-selected subset.

1.bcz.bz/5r
Interact

Because we wish to prove the node has been in communication with many other nodes, and also to guarantee every node has a fair opportunity to add to its participation score, we impose a **peer filter** on the receipts which may be included in a block. Periodically, the network pseudo-randomly computes a new network topology that governs which peers a given node is allowed to publish receipts from. Unlike the data filter, this filter is assumed to be known by all nodes at the beginning of each new topology period, to ensure that nodes have a fair chance to reorganize their peer connections to collect the receipts they will be allowed to publish in the future.

1.bcz.bz/5s
Interact

A receipt is only worth a higher participation score if the publishing node can prove that the receipt was a member of a commitment (receipt Merkle root) already included in a previously published receipt, proving that the new receipt that matches these filters existed before the filter criteria were known. When such a proof accompanies a receipt in a block, it is defined as a **linked** receipt.

1.bcz.bz/5t
Interact

If a node does not have any receipts to link, it can still include un-linked receipts (not included in a Merkle root published by another node in a previous receipt) to earn a much lower score. While these receipts prove little about the publishing node, they do include commitments from their creators, and can later be used to prove pre-existence when those creators publish and link their own receipts.

1.bcz.bz/5u
Interact

In order to compute the change in participation score, we assign each block a value by counting a small number of points for each un-linked receipt and a larger number of points for each linked receipt. There is a fixed maximum number of receipts which can be included in a block, so we can clearly state that the maximum block value is given for a block filled with linked receipts, and the minimum block value (0) is given for a block with no receipts.

1.bcz.bz/5v
Interact

If the total value for the block exceeds half of the maximum block value, the creating node's participation score will increase for this block; otherwise it will decrease. Should a node miss its turn to create a block entirely, it will forfeit twice the amount of a participation score as if it had produced a block with zero receipts.

1.bcz.bz/5w
Interact

The Receipt Object

Field	Size	Description
Sender Public Key	32 bytes	The public key of the sending node
Receiver Public Key	32 bytes	The public key of the receiving node
Data Type	4 bytes	A code indicating the type of datum that was sent (Block, Transaction, File Chunk, etc.)
Data Hash	32 bytes	The hash of the datum that was sent
Ref Block Height	4 bytes	The height of a recent reference block
Ref Block Hash	32 bytes	The hash of the recent reference block at the height specified
Receipt Merkle Root	32 bytes	A Merkle root of receipt objects previously received by the sending node
Receiver Signature	32 bytes	The digital signature of the receiving node (receipt producer) on all of the above data
Total	**200 bytes**	

Producing Receipts

When a node transmits some piece of data to another node (such as a transaction or block), the receiving node (after validating the data) should produce a receipt object and return it to the sender. This receipt should be created and returned regardless of whether the receiving node had already received and rebroadcast the same data from another node, so long as the data itself is valid.

1.bcz.bz/5x
Interact

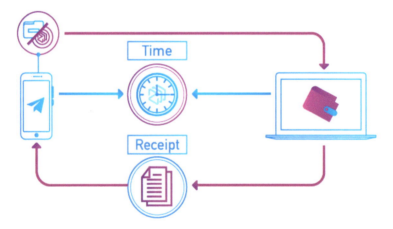

The receiving node will populate the "Sender Public Key" with the public key of the node which sent it the data, and the "Receiver Public Key" with its own node public key. "Data Type" is filled with a type code stating whether the data is a block, transaction or potentially other kinds of transmission, and the "Data Hash" field is filled with the hash of the data item which was transmitted. "Ref Block Height" is filled with the node's current block height, and "Ref Block Hash" with the hash of the block at that block height.

To fill the "Receipt Merkle Root", the receiving node will look up a recent Merkle root in its "batch table" (described below). While the content of this Merkle root field cannot be validated by other nodes, it is in the receiver's interest to include a proper commitment which he can later use to prove the prior existence of other receipts he has collected.

1.bcz.bz/5y
Interact

Finally, the node signs all the above data with its private key, guaranteeing the receipt could not be produced without its involvement. The receipt object is then sent back to the node which transmitted the data. Repeated failure to return a valid receipt object may result in the sending node blacklisting the receiving node.

1.bcz.bz/5z
Interact

Collecting Receipts

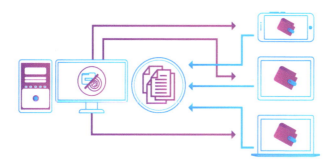

As a node broadcasts pieces of data to other nodes, it will collect and save the receipts that are returned from each receiving node These receipts are organized into **batches,** and a Merkle root is calculated for each batch which can be included in future receipts produced by the node.

The number of receipts which we allow to be proven by a single Merkle root is limited, therefore it is not in the node's interest to save any receipts that it already knows will not be usable later. The node can safely discard any receipts that it already knows will not be permitted to include in a future block, in particular receipts which do not match its peer filter.

1.bcz.bz/62
Interact

The maximum batch size is governed by a constant defined in the protocol **rmr max depth,** being the maximum allowed depth of a receipt Merkle tree. Functionally, this translates into the maximum number of intermediate hashes a node is allowed to publish along with a receipt to prove its membership in a previously published Merkle root.

1.bcz.bz/63
Interact

Receipts only need to be collected in memory by a node (i.e. not written to the hard drive) until the node is ready to finalize the batch and then write them to the database. When it is time to finalize the batch, the node will first compute the Merkle root of all the receipts in the batch and save a new record in the batch table, connecting the root to the block height at which it was created.

The node then adds all of the receipts included in the batch to the receipt table. Each record in the receipt table will specify the batch ID (Merkle root) that the receipt belongs to, and also its sequence number within the batch.

In this way, as the node collects receipts, it keeps a personal record of all the information it will later need to find out if one of its commitments has been published by another node and to construct the necessary proof (or "link") that some of its receipts were previously committed.

1.bcz.bz/66
Interact

Batch Table Structure

Field	Type	Description
Batch Merkle Root	32-byte blob	The Merkle root of all receipts included in this batch
Created Height	4-byte int	The block height when this batch was created

Receipt Table Structure

Field	Type	Description
Batch ID	8-byte int	The first 8 bytes of the batch Merkle root
Seq Number	4-byte int	This receipt's position within its batch
Receipt Hash	32-byte blob	The pre-calculated hash of the receipt object
[Receipt Data]		The full data of the receipt object structured the same way as the receipt object specified above

Pruning Old Receipts

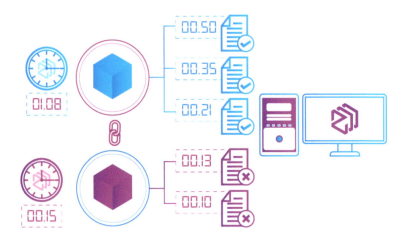

As all receipts have an expiration time (based on the block height they include), there is no benefit in keeping them forever. Additionally, each batch stores the block height from when it was created, making it easy to detect when all the receipts within a batch have expired. These expired receipts can be safely deleted.

The node will run a pruning process which occasionally checks if there are expired batches and cleans them from the database. Therefore, the entire receipt storage process should fit in a constant memory footprint, cleaning the old ones as new ones are accumulated.

1.bcz.bz/67
Interact

Proving Linked Receipts

When a receipt is included in a block, it can either be un-linked (meaning its prior existence cannot be proven by any Merkle root previously published) or linked (when prior existence can be proven.)

1.bcz.bz/68
Interact

When a node wishes to link a receipt, it must include a set of intermediate hashes which, when hashed in sequence with the hash of the receipt, yield a Merkle root hash which has been previously published in a block.

1.bcz.bz/69
Interact

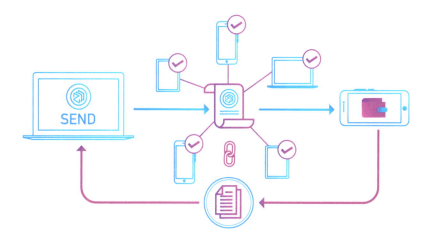

In order to do this, when constructing a block, the node will first compare the set of receipt Merkle roots it has stored to all recently published receipt Merkle roots, and begin searching through any receipts it possesses which are already included in one of these previous Merkle roots.

When it finds a receipt that matches the filter criteria for receipts in the new block it is creating, the node can use the precomputed set of intermediate hashes composing that Merkle Root to look up which intermediate hashes it must include with the new receipt to prove the linkage.

1.bcz.bz/6a
Interact

In practice, proving the link is quite straightforward: first, hash the receipt. Then, find the hash of the string made of that receipt hash concatenated with the first provided intermediate hash. Then, hash the obtained result concatenated with the next provided intermediate hash. Repeat this step for all provided intermediate hashes. If the result at the end precisely matches a recently published Merkle root, this proves the receipt object must have already existed at the time when the Merkle root was created, and the link is valid. If it matches none, then the block creator has tried to forge a link where none exists, hence the entire block becomes invalid.

1.bcz.bz/6b
Interact

The Height Filter

As described above, each receipt to be included in a block must be valid according to different filters, which are parameterized when the block is being created and can be objectively validated by other nodes when they receive the block. The simplest of these is the *height filter.*

Each published receipt contains a block height and the corresponding hash of the block at that height. It is possible to craft a receipt that specifies an earlier block height than when it was produced, but it is not possible to produce a valid receipt for a future block height, as this would require foreknowledge of the block hash at that future height. Therefore, we can say that a receipt was created no later than the block height at which it was created and signed.

1.bcz.bz/6d
Interact

Each time a node is added or removed from the registry, the network recomputes the receipt expiration time, which is the maximum difference allowed between the block height at which a receipt was created and the block height at which it is published. When a receipt is selected to be published, the node will compare its age to the receipt expiration time to determine its validity, and other nodes will confirm this when they validate the receipts published in the new block.

In order to maintain or increase its participation score, a node must reliably publish linked receipts. To give a node a fair chance to survive in the registry, the receipt expiration time must be greater than the average expected time between a previous block publishing one of its receipts and the node being allowed to publish a receipt that links to it.

1.bcz.bz/6f
Interact

For this reason, the expiration time is computed as a function of the registry size, as the number of nodes in the lottery to create blocks can be used to determine the average chance that a certain number of receipts from a node have been previously published within a given timeframe. We will continue to experiment with this function through our alpha and beta network testing to reach the best algorithm to keep this timeframe secure.

1.bcz.bz/6g
Interact

The Peer Filter

The most complex filter imposed on receipts is the **peer filter.** The first objective of this filter is to require that each node in the registry connects to a diversity of other nodes and that the selection of these preferred peers is random and beyond its control. This minimizes an attacker's ability to selectively favor his own other nodes with the Proof of Participation algorithm, as on average he would need to control almost all of the registry and withhold his participation from all of the remaining nodes in order to eventually create a more valid chain.

1.bcz.bz/6h
Interact

We divide time into **network topology periods** of 60 blocks. Every 60 blocks, the network will pseudo-randomly compute an ordering of all nodes in the registry and use this ordering to assign a set of preferred peers to each node. Each node can easily compute its own preferred peers and connect to them in favor of others. More importantly, when the node publishes receipts later, the receipts it is allowed to publish must come from one of its assigned peers at the time the receipt was created.

1.bcz.bz/6j
Interact

The second objective of the filter, closely connected with the first, is to ensure that each node in the registry has a fair chance to have their previous receipts published. This helps create some statistical certainty and uniformity in how many blocks we can expect on average between any given node's receipts being published, which helps guarantee that even honest nodes do not make their receipt selections in a way that accidentally excludes some other honest node.

1.bcz.bz/6k
Interact

Beyond the above properties, this preferred peer assignment strategy also gives us the opportunity to optimally organize the peer-to-peer network topology of nodes in the registry. By optimally, we mean that assuming all nodes are online, for a network size N, and a number of preferred peers P, we can guarantee that a new transmission is gossiped to the entire network in a maximum of H hops, computed:

1.bcz.bz/6m
Interact

$$H = \text{ceil} \left(\log_P \left(N \right) \right)$$

For example, if each node has 20 assigned peers to broadcast to, even in a registry of 50,000 nodes, the broadcast will reach all nodes after only 4 hops.

While decentralization prevents us from forcing any given peer to follow this preferred peer assignment, it creates a strong crypto-economic incentive for nodes to comply with this connection strategy: if they do not collect receipts from their assigned peers in a given time period, they will be unable to publish receipts later which pass the peer filter, and subsequently their participation score will fall, reducing the amount of coinbase rewards they will collect and eventually ejecting them from the node registry altogether.

1.bcz.bz/6n
Interact

The Data Filter

The two filters above are known in advance to the node collecting receipts, and a node could pass them by only transmitting a few pieces of data to each of its peers during each network topology period. Because we wish to incentivize nodes to transmit all relevant data, we impose a **data filter** on the receipts that can be published in a block, such that only receipts for a small random subset of all data recently transmitted may be included in a given block.

1.bcz.bz/6p
Interact

In practice, the node keeps count of the number of blocks and transactions that have been published since the receipt expiration time. (This counts only transactions included in blocks, so the number for a given block height is strictly in consensus for all nodes.) This number is used to calculate a filter width, a number between 0 and 1, which represents the likelihood that the hash of any given block or transaction is good to be published in a new block.

1.bcz.bz/6q
Interact

A receipt passes the data filter if, for the BlockSeed and FilterWidth at block height H, and for the DataHash of a receipt R, the following condition is true:

$$(\text{hash} (\text{BlockSeed}_H + \text{DataHash}_R) [8] / (2\text{\textasciicircum}64)) < \text{FilterWidth}_H$$

Therefore, in order to have a reasonable chance of being able to provide enough receipts to pass the data filter when called on to produce a block, a node must collect receipts for all data transmissions occuring during this period.

1.bcz.bz/6r
Interact

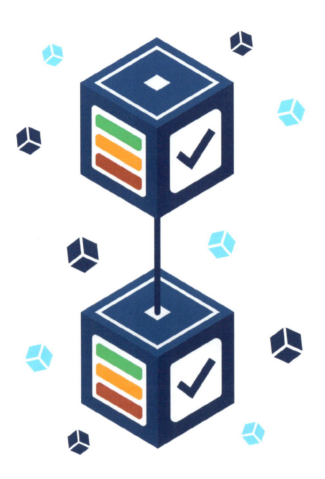

A Chain Reaction

1.bcz.bz/47
Interact

Scan to discuss this
chapter online

What started out as an idea between two people had quickly expanded to a team of 20+, diligently working on our new blockchain.

We had begun with the foundational programming and structuring of the blockchain itself, hoping to get each individual piece running smoothly and from there teach them how to seamlessly interact with one another. To do this, we needed to make each piece talk to one another to start testing, and then see what was working or not working.

We divided everyone into different teams, and they all had individual projects while maintaining the global view of our goal. To assemble the blockchain, we needed multiple pieces set up and running smoothly. For instance, we needed a piece that produced the block, another that validated peer-to-peer networks, others that validated the consensus mechanism, and pieces that validated transactions.

By this point, all those pieces had not yet been put together in order to have a working node of the blockchain. In addition, two of our other focuses were on building the spine blocks and the snapshot shortcuts. We knew we needed the spine blocks to make up the initial infrastructure of the blockchain, but we also needed the snapshot shortcuts to help with scaling.

What many software developers don't initially realize is that blockchain prototypes require so many facets of fully realized software components, before you can test them to see if anything will work. There's no way to create a single piece and then look at the whole project, while having full confidence in its outcome.

You have to start small, take those first successes to heart, and keep your eye on the big picture. Everything needs to communicate, everything needs to intersect, and everything needs to stay entirely secure, at every turn. You need to have that true blockchain prototype fully realized, with all its components intact, before you can start testing and looking toward the next steps.

Once we had the initial prototype up and running, our confidence settled into place. It finally felt like this was going to work. That being said, we still hadn't figured out how we were going to do Proof of Participation (PoP). We just kind of held out on faith that we were gonna figure it out.

We had a rough idea at that time, but no executable plan. We wouldn't have a smoothly working version of the PoP mechanism until we started developing the real thing, several months later.

Coinbase Distribution

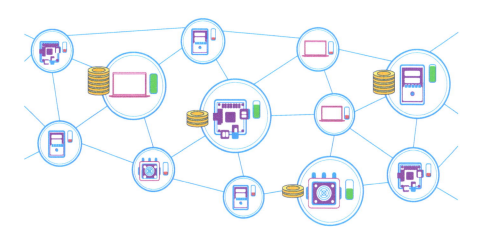

Conventionally, only the node which produces a block on the network is rewarded with newly minted tokens. If the network becomes very large, the chance that any given node will produce a block (especially one with a lower participation score) within a specific period, and therefore receive a reward, diminishes.

One of our major objectives with the Node Registration and Proof of Participation algorithms is to more fairly reward the full set of network participants, and to do so in a more timely manner. In keeping with this goal, we implement a pseudo-random lottery to reward many accounts per block, with participants' chances to win being weighted by their participation score.

1.bcz.bz/6t
Interact

Here we detail how we compute the amount of new tokens minted per block and how they are distributed to network participants.

Coinbase Schedule

Styled after Bitcoin, many blockchains offer a fixed reward per block for some period of blocks, after which the reward amount is cut in half for the next period, and so on. This geometric reduction ensures that the earlier participants are rewarded more than the later ones, and also that the number of tokens produced will approach, but not exceed, a target total supply.

We feel it is cleaner to define a smooth curve across all blocks rather than explicit halving events, such that the number of new tokens produced by a block is a simple function of its block height. For this curve, we take a window of a common sigmoid function:

1.bcz.bz/6v
Interact

$$1 / (1 + e^{(-x)})$$

Where **x** ranges from approximately **2-6**, while we still evaluate the parameters. This window is stretched over a period of **180 months (15 years)** to give the coinbase curve.

We prefer a function of this form over a pure logarithmic curve (which other networks such as Bitcoin approximate with periodic halvings) because as a pure curve, this would yield an inordinate number of coins released in the first few years, which we would prefer to leave for later participants.

1.bcz.bz/6w
Interact

Based on this rate of distribution, ZooBC expects to reach a target supply of 33,333,333 tokens over 15 years (the exact values will be evaluated and announced before the beta version goes online).

1.bcz.bz/6x
Interact

Total Distributed Vs Per Month

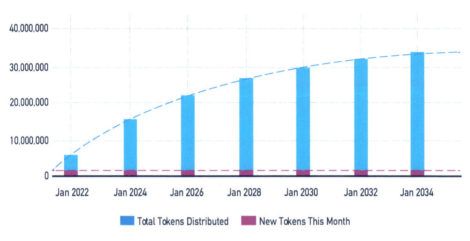

Example token distribution based on the logistic function, using window x={3...6}

Recipient Selection

For each block, a list of coinbase recipients is computed deterministically from the current state of the node registry and the new block's seed. We define an **ordering function** to compute a pseudo-random number for each node, weighted by its participation score, then select up to a maximum of X nodes with the lowest computed order numbers.

Where hash is the first 8 bytes of a SHA3-512 hash, PK_N is the public key of node N, PS_N is the pop score of node N, and BS_H is the first 8 bytes of the block seed at height H, we give the ordering function as:

1.bcz.bz/6y
Interact

$$order_N = hash(hash(BS_H) + PK_N) * (1 / PS_N)$$

Once we have computed this list of winners, the total block reward available according to the provided coinbase schedule function is divided evenly between the winners, with the newly minted tokens being credited to the winning node's associated account.

1.bcz.bz/6z
Interact

It is worth noting that the Proof of Participation score has a fixed maximum, which any good node should attain after some time. Therefore, in a large network of good nodes, rewards should be frequent, fairly distributed, and not directly tied to recent block production, provided that the node keeps participating.

1.bcz.bz/72
Interact

Why does ZooBC blockchain use the **SHA-3** hashing algorithm instead of **SHA-2**?

Overcoming Roadblocks

1.bcz.bz/48
Interact

Scan to discuss this
chapter online

If you ask any small business about their startup story, it'll sound something like a dystopian nightmare. Here at Blockchain Zoo, we found ourselves incredibly fortunate from day one. We hired a network of blockchain developers that are as committed to our mission of technological agnosticism as we are, and therefore found ourselves with a dedicated team of problem solvers.

From the beginning, we were busy helping our clientele implement blockchain solutions and spent a great deal of our time in consultations, teaching people not only what blockchain is and how it works, but how it could work for them as an individual and as a company. blockchain Zoo began with the goal of researching and producing blockchain applications that are simple enough for anyone to learn and use in their daily lives. We knew from the get-go that when people were introduced to blockchain, it was usually in the realm of finance.

That being said, we didn't focus on finance, instead, we have been dedicating our efforts to the decentralized systems that had other functions, like document management, titles, etc. We also knew how much misinformation exists around blockchain technology. So in the process of combating the myths and misunderstandings, we realized there were real issues that needed solving within the field of blockchain, which simply didn't exist yet.

As fate would have it, in June of 2019, we found ourselves at an interesting crossroads. Our current clients' projects had wrapped up at nearly the same moment, and all of our developers were available for new projects. We decided to go all-in, and the ZooBC project was born.

Before this point, ZooBC, and the solutions to common blockchain problems we had visualized, were merely a twinkle in the company's eye. When it comes to decentralized systems, there are a few core problems that have needed addressing for some time now. We saw this challenge and decided to split our group of blockchain developers into three teams, each with a unique focus that required them to work in parallel with one another.

One team was focused on wallet-related hardware and software, with the main goal of developing and implementing all the needed functionality for web wallet, and mobile wallets. This had the potential of including things down the line like hardware signing devices, browser extensions, and interface with eID card readers. The second team was assigned to build the explorer software, as well as being responsible for supporting and maintaining the network.

Lastly, but arguably most importantly, we had a team dedicated to the node core software, which needed many pieces to be fully implemented before the first two teams could make consistent progress. Once the node core team was past the point of developing the basic infrastructure, all three teams could move at a parallel pace. That was probably the biggest challenge to overcome.

Within a year we went from point A to the near-completion of ZooBC, and we couldn't be more excited.

Spine Blocks

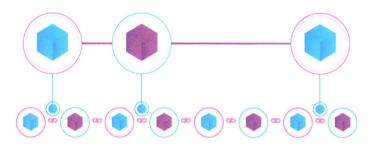

Once a day, the ZooBC architecture creates a special block called a *spine block*, also chained to the previous spine block. These blocks form a set of hops that allow a node to skip regular blocks following the spine blocks from the genesis block to the current time. This provides a fast route to any moment in the history of the blockchain. Spine blocks are created once per day on average and contain the major updates to the node registry (which nodes joined and which left) and other metadata but contain no transactions, resulting in an extremely light set of blocks to download.

1.bcz.bz/73
Interact

In this way, a node only needs to download a very light block for each day of the life of the blockchain, having a constant up-to-date list of who was in the node registry at each moment in the history of ZooBC, and so can evaluate if the next spine block has been created by a legitimate node. This allows, in the case of a fork, a new node to choose the best spine block between several options presented.

1.bcz.bz/74
Interact

The first step for any new node is to download, starting at the genesis block, all the spine blocks (choosing, in case of a fork, the set of blocks with the highest cumulative difficulty) until it arrives at the latest available spine block. The node then uses the most recent blockchain snapshot hash found in a spine block (more on this below) to identify and download a blockchain snapshot from peers on the network. This allows a new node to come up to date with the live blockchain in a few minutes, even if ZooBC has run for decades and the blockchain has a collective weight of many gigabytes of data.

1.bcz.bz/75
Interact

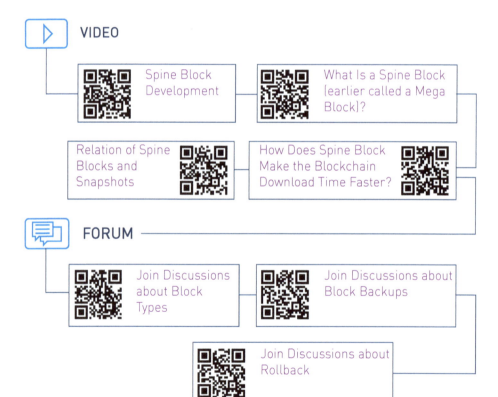

VIDEO

Spine Block Development

What Is a Spine Block (earlier called a Mega Block)?

Relation of Spine Blocks and Snapshots

How Does Spine Block Make the Blockchain Download Time Faster?

FORUM

Join Discussions about Block Types

Join Discussions about Block Backups

Join Discussions about Rollback

ZOOBC Q&A

 Get Your Questions about Spine Blocks Answered

Structure of a Spine Block

Unlike regular blocks on the blockchain, in which the block creator can select which transactions and receipts should be included, the contents of a spine block (all except for the set of digital signatures needed to create and validate the spine block) are purely determined by the state of the blockchain. Therefore, any node in consensus will produce precisely the same spine block that any other node would produce at the same block height.

1.bcz.bz/76
Interact

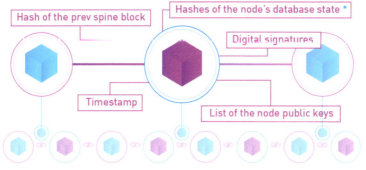

Hash of the prev spine block

Hashes of the node's database state *

Digital signatures

Timestamp

List of the node public keys

* All the other days of the month no snapshot hash is included in the spine block.

A spine block first contains the hash of the previous spine block, and a timestamp, just like a normal blockchain's block. This is the essence of any blockchain and guarantees that the older blocks have not been tampered with.

Each spine block also contains a list of node public keys which have been added to, or removed from, the node registry since the last spine block. As the node applies spine blocks in sequence, the set of additions and removals tracks a "key pool" which roughly follows the set of node public keys in the node registry. '

1.bcz.bz/77
Interact

Each spine block must contain a collection of digital signatures on its contents. The set of keys which may legally sign, and how much value each of their signatures contributes to the cumulative difficulty of the spine block, are governed by the consensus mechanism described below.

Finally, approximately once per month, based on the rules for when database snapshots are taken (see below), it is OK for the spine block creator to include the hashes of the node's database state. All the other days of the month no snapshot hash is included in the spine block. Details on how this snapshot is created are presented in the section below on Snapshots.

1.bcz.bz/79
Interact

Signature Accumulation

Every node in consensus will generate the same spine block at the same moment, so we need a mechanism to govern which node will broadcast the spine block first, and how it will accumulate signatures from other nodes in the key pool.

In the same way that potential next block creators are selected from the node registry, after each spine block, a priority list of next signers is calculated. To be valid, the new spine block must collect the signatures of a large number of these nodes. The higher on the priority list the signers, the greater the "cumulative difficulty" of the spine block. In this way only an attacker who controls more than 90% of the nodes in the registry can be lucky enough to create a set of spine blocks with a greater cumulative difficulty (and therefore more authority) than the honest set of spine blocks.

1.bcz.bz/7b
Interact

Nodes then undergo a process of gossiping signatures on the new spine block to each other, until enough are collected to consider the spine block confirmed, and assign it a cumulative difficulty score according to the priority position of the signers in the randomized list. At this time, the hash of the new spine block is finalized, and it is broadcast along with all collected signatures to the rest of the network.

Just as with regular blocks, if there are two competing versions of the spine block sets available, the node will always select the one which has the higher cumulative difficulty score.

1.bcz.bz/7c
Interact

Joining the Network

When a new node connects to the ZooBC network, it will first reach out to the well-known peers it is configured with. From these, it will continue through a period of network discovery by querying peers from elsewhere until it has a sizable collection.

The node will first query the hash and height of the last spine block from this set of peers. If there are multiple candidate sets of spine blocks, it will first select the set reporting the highest cumulative difficulty. The node will then download all the spine blocks from its connected peers, starting at the genesis block, confirming that the cumulative difficulty claimed by the last spine block is legitimate.

After arriving at the latest spine block, the node looks backward to find the latest registered snapshot hash. The node can then compute (as a function of the snapshot hash and the current state of the node registry) which nodes maintain this snapshot and begin downloading it from them.

Once the snapshot is downloaded and hashed to confirm its legitimacy, the node will import the contents into its current database state. This brings the node up-to-date with the state of the blockchain at the block height when the snapshot was created. From there, the node simply downloads from the network the remaining blocks as usual to catch up to the current state of the network.

In other blockchains, the blocks that a node needs to download to validate the current state of the blockchain are those with all the transactions from the genesis (block 0) to the latest block height. In ZooBC, a node can shortcut to the most recent archived state through the spine blocks, and only downloading the full blocks of the time since the last snapshot (at the most would be a month's worth of blocks).

1.bcz.bz/7h
Interact

▷ **VIDEO**

What Nodes Can Validate
Spine Blocks?

Everybody Loves an Alpha

1.bcz.bz/4b
Interact

Scan to discuss this
chapter online

The moment that our alpha was ready to go, we set up a small blockchain with Raspberry Pis as nodes, as the code itself is super lightweight and can run on small devices. We ran more than one node on each Raspberry Pi, and before we knew it, we had a network of them running the blockchain and producing blocks! We were even able to send transactions back and forth. Everything was working.

That being said, at this point the alpha had very few of the planned features from our white paper implemented. However, it did have enough features to run the blockchain, send tokens from one node to another, and register nodes. Even more exciting, the Proof of Participation mechanism was in place and running smoothly.

Between that and getting the block creation algorithm in place, we were becoming more and more hopeful. We had our 100 nodes set up and interacting with one another, at the same time that the tests were coming along nicely. Everything was working, as we had anticipated and hoped it would.

The tests themselves mainly consisted of analyzing the network as a whole, rather than how every node was affected by each newly-added feature. With a blockchain network, you have to think about it holistically, you can't keep your focus on the tiny details. This holistic approach is in fact necessary for all kinds of decentralized projects.

We could compare it to the human body. There are lots of different cell types, and someone may be able to tell how the cells work individually in great detail, and which ones are doing a great job. But it is only after those cells are next to each other, and it can be observed how they form an organism, that there is a full picture of whether they function correctly. The same is true with blockchain nodes.

Since the release of the alpha, we had been examining "the full organism," the full network, and that helped us ensure that we were on track. It kept us honest with ourselves and our associates, not letting us be fooled into a false sense of progress. We need to always know that we're making progress, and we need to know when something's not going to work in a decentralized setting.

The wallet of the user, in ZooBC, needs to be able to manage a node within the network of the blockchain. Also, some transaction types we have implemented don't exist in other blockchains. This has been a unique challenge to configure each transaction type properly, as some are not broadcasted on the blockchain. That way it goes straight from wallet to node, as it sets the configuration and the set account IDs.

As we continued, our alpha was finally up and running, our nodes were interacting, and our transactions were running smoothly. It was time to update the world about our progress!

Snapshots

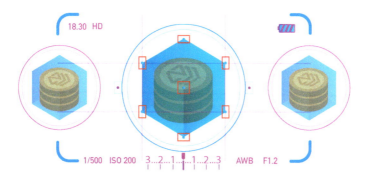

One of our objectives is to reduce the blockchain download time to a constant (or nearly so). The blockchain download time is a notorious problem, as traditionally each node must download and apply in sequence the entire history of previous blocks and transactions before it can begin evaluating the validity of new transactions, and the size of this historical record necessarily continues to grow for the lifetime of the chain.

To give an example: at the time of writing (18th November 2019), the Bitcoin blockchain, almost 11 years old (the genesis block is dated 9th January 2009), weighs 291GB, while the Ethereum blockchain, almost 4 and a half years old (the genesis block is dated 30th July 2015), weighs almost double: 455GB (equivalent to downloading 350 high definition movies). See https://bitinfocharts.com for more info on blockchain's data.

To address the blockchain bloat issue, in ZooBC, each node periodically (at a block height agreed by the network) takes a snapshot of the current state of its database, and computes a set of hashes for this snapshot. To be sure the node has the same snapshot as all the other nodes, it compares its new snapshot hashes against the hashes of the snapshot as calculated with the hashes in the metadata of a new spine block proposed by a blocksmith.

1.bcz.bz/7m
Interact

If the blocksmith uses hashes that, combined with known snapshot hashes, lead to the same set of hashes the majority of nodes in the node registry has calculated, its block is approved; otherwise it is rejected. Any new node joining the network then only needs to download the spine blocks until it finds the block with the hashes of the latest database snapshot, and downloads it in chunks from its peers, to come up to a recent database state, from which it can finish downloading the most recent blocks to catch up to the rest of the network.

The maximum size of a completely new snapshot can be determined by the sum of all the assets and accounts with current balance and relative properties. To produce a valid number in Mb we need to wait for the beta version to be running and do stress tests to the blockchain.

1.bcz.bz/7p
Interact

VIDEO

 How Snapshot Works in ZooBC

 What ZooBC Blocks Store the Snapshots?

What Is Snapshot Time Interval?

Relation between Spine Blocks and Snapshots

 FORUM

 Join Discussions about Snapshot

 ZOOBC Q&A

 Get Your Questions about Snapshot Answered

Creating Snapshots

———

Approximately once per month, all nodes deterministically select a block height at which the next database snapshot should be taken. Each node will wait until enough blocks have elapsed that they have surpassed the "maximum rollback height", in order to guard against instances where the node begins computing the snapshot and then must abandon this to process a rollback **(see glossary in Appendix 3 at page 218)**.

1.bcz.bz/7q
Interact

At this point the node initiates a background process to begin constructing a file that represents the exact state of the node's database from the earlier block height determined to be the snapshot height. Once this file is constructed, it is saved as a snapshot, and its hashes are computed.

In order to give nodes time to construct the snapshot file, a grace period of many more blocks is given before it becomes legal to include the new snapshot hash into a spine block. This ensures that once the new spine block is broadcast, all nodes, even those running on very limited hardware such as an Arduino or Raspberry Pi, should be able to construct and hash their snapshot file, and thereby validate the hashes in the new spine block against the one they independently computed.

1.bcz.bz/7r
Interact

Beating the Blockchain Blues

1.bcz.bz/4d
Interact

Scan to discuss this
chapter online

At this point, we had dedicated months of our lives to this project, poured our hearts and souls into it, and even bet our business on it. Yet the moment had finally arrived. It was time to show our blockchain to other people.

As we embarked on showing ZooBC to our peers and associates, we readied ourselves for some of the feedback that would then launch us onto the next phase of development. We put ourselves and our project out there, and... got crickets in response.

The constructive criticism that we did receive was mainly due to a misunderstanding of the functionality of our blockchain, and once that was clarified, it was back to silence. People saw it, they seemed to understand it, but something wasn't clicking. We realized we needed to change our approach to how we were educating and informing people.

We took the first draft of our white paper and found places and spaces where we could discuss ZooBC and the Proof of Participation mechanism. We figured out that we needed to talk to people who had a preexisting interest in blockchain. Otherwise, a lot of our information was falling on ears that were too busy learning to keep up and certainly too confused to offer constructive feedback on the project itself.

The skeleton document of the white paper was very bare-bones. We had essentially written a list of the algorithms we were using and explained them to people. We were discussing the problem with other consensus mechanisms and blockchains, as well as how we planned to solve those pain points with ZooBC. Once our presentation changed, everything was easier to communicate.

Next, we set up 50 nodes to begin stress testing the network. All 50 seemed to be working fine, so we decided to move to 100 nodes sparsely spread all over the world. Once the 100 nodes were introduced to the blockchain, everything shut down. The code seemed to be fine, but there was an issue with the mechanics that allowed different nodes to talk to, and understand, one another.

We were so grateful for that test because it was the true moment where we started to figure out the practical needs of running the blockchain. When building it, there are so many potential possibilities that you simply don't know what the network is going to need, until it needs it.

A great deal of our work from there turned into fixing, patching, and editing the blockchain until it ran smoothly and securely. This constant need for our attention, as well as our updates to the software, put us about a year behind schedule. But it was so worth it. We had something that we knew was special, so getting it right was well worth the time and effort.

Block Backups

State snapshots allow a node to zoom to the current state of major intervals in the blockchain's history. However, in order to rebuild the database state at any particular block height, a record must still be kept of all previous blocks and transactions. Additionally, in some cases the information in a transaction itself (not the resulting database state) may be required by a user, such as a digitally signed message.

In the same way that a node produces large snapshot files, it will also periodically produce files which contain sets of blocks, transactions, and receipts, from a particular range of block heights, that need to be archived. Another node that wishes to inspect or replay these blocks, after they have been archived and pruned from its own database, may request from other nodes to download the needed blocks backup file.

If we assume all nodes keep all block backups, this may seem like an equivalent (or worse) strategy to having the node simply store all historical blocks in the blockchain. But combined with a general mechanism for sharding the storage of large files across nodes on the network (described below), this allows for major space savings.

1.bcz.bz/7u
Interact

 FORUM

 Join Discussions about Block Backups

Permission to Play

1.bcz.bz/4t
Interact

Scan to discuss this
chapter online

When you create something completely new, you need to focus a lot of your energy on teaching people new information. Everyone has sat through a class or a meeting at some point in their life where they've thought to themselves, "get me out of here." We wanted to avoid that feeling in our clients and users at all costs, so we dedicated ourselves to mixing up the learning process.

One of our developers surprised us by creating a video game that interacted with the ZooBC interface, allowing people to both learn about, and use, ZooBC in an intuitive and interesting setting. We knew we wanted to create a way to visually teach and entertain new users, but the video game concept made these dreams a reality.

We know that we live in a multimedia era. Now more than ever, it's important to inspire people, motivate them, and show them exactly why what we're doing is worthwhile. If they can see it in action, they are much more likely to have a meaningful, emotional connection to it. So one of our biggest goals became creating a visual, media-driven interpretation of the inner workings of ZooBC.

With that in mind, we created a competition on the ZooBC blockchain. Every time there is space for a node to be added to the registry, a small competition is run to determine exactly which node gets added next. One of our ideas revolved around visualizing this competition as a kind of auto race where the individual cars, each representing a single node, would be racing one another.

We wanted something that allowed everyone to see who's in the lead, and therefore incentivizing people to have fun keeping on top of their participation, and trying to make sure that their node was going to win the race. We had other race-based ideas, like a balloon race, a horse race, and different types of auto races. At this stage though, we were pretty focused on the car racing idea. We specifically thought about visualizations that correlated to the new node registration process.

Think about it like a popular club with a lot of people inside, and a line of people outside waiting to get in. We needed something to act like a bouncer that decides if you're going to be good to enter, and if not, throws you out. We thought a game that required participation from the get-go would be a great way to keep people interested, and invested, as they were waiting to register.

Game on!

File Distribution

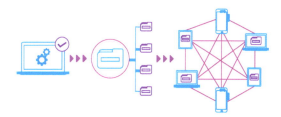

It is important that the network remembers old state snapshots and block backups in a decentralized way, both because new nodes need to catch up to the network without a central point of truth, and because a node operator may want to go backward in time and validate an old transaction in the context in which it happened, or recover other states which only existed at a particular time.

Every node keeps the full data of the two latest snapshots in order to make them maximally available to new nodes joining the network. However, after this time, it is overly redundant for them to be duplicated across all nodes. Therefore we employ a strategy similar to the Torrent protocol, to fairly divide the work of storing old snapshots and block backups.

1.bcz.bz/7w
Interact

Each file is subdivided into smaller chunks, and the responsibility for which set of nodes in the registry should retain each chunk is computed deterministically. As a network parameter, we specify only the number of redundant copies of each chunk that the network should maintain, and the chunk assignment algorithm automatically updates this responsibility when nodes enter or leave the registry.

1.bcz.bz/7x
Interact

When a set of nodes is chosen to be the custodian of certain chunks of the files, there is no need for those chunks to be transmitted, meaning that other nodes can delete those chunks to free up space on their hard drives. These files are generated locally the same way by each node and only need to be transmitted to another node upon request. This saves most network traffic compared to the Torrent protocol (on which ZooBC's decentralized storage is modeled), where a single peer posts a file and other peers download chunks from it to keep redundancy of the file in the network.

1.bcz.bz/7y
Interact

When a node wishes to retrieve a large file, such as a snapshot from the network, it will first query other nodes with the hash of that file for a manifest of the hashes of the chunks which compose the file. For each chunk hash, the node can compute which set of registered nodes are currently responsible for storing that chunk, and it can pick one at random from which to download it. Once all the chunks have been collected, they can be assembled and hashed together, and the final hash can be verified against the requested file hash.

1.bcz.bz/7z
Interact

ZooBC computes the number of redundant copies of any chunk as the square root of the registry size. In this way, as the network grows, more redundant copies of each chunk are maintained, but the number of copies grows more slowly than the size of the network, therefore the burden of each node on average continues to be reduced (adding nodes to the network reduces the storage responsibility of any given node).

1.bcz.bz/82
Interact

Founding Fathers & Mothers: A New Type of Fundraising

1.bcz.bz/4u
Interact

Scan to discuss this
chapter online

Fundraising in the blockchain world is either really hard, or really easy — no in-betweens. The former because if you don't do an ICO (initial coin offering) you have to fundraise the normal way: through hard work, effective marketing, and a solid business model that excites investors.

The latter because, as the 2017 craze showed us, virtually anyone with an idea (or a scam) that was related to blockchain and cryptocurrencies could run a successful ICO. This type of fundraising was rampant for over a year, with newly-founded blockchain companies raking in tens, or even hundreds, of millions of investors' money. Though many of them had no products.

All these companies had to do was add a blockchain element to an already existing industry — such as music, sports, or hairdressing — then create a nice looking website with successful sounding founders and advisors, while largely copying the white papers of more renowned crypto companies, and promising incredible returns for being the "Bitcoin" of that industry.

At Blockchain Zoo, we knew that this type of fundraising was a no-go. Not only did we not want to do an ICO, or an ITO (initial token offering), which required pre-mined coins or tokens. We also did not want to fuel the misconception that blockchains are just about returns for investors. We actually wanted to reward the users — for their participation — not investors.

So instead of using a proof-of-stake chain, where a billion coins can be created at the genesis block to be distributed to investors, we respected the original spirit of Bitcoin founder, Satoshi Nakamoto. This meant no coins existed at the beginning of the blockchain, until every block advanced — distributing the newly-created tokens among the nodes supporting the blockchain.

This was great, in theory. But how could we get the "crypto whales" (6+ figure investors) to be interested in our nascent project if the prospects of riches weren't there from the beginning?

One of the bigger novelties brought by ZooBC is its unique consensus mechanism: the Proof of Participation. Unlike Proof of Stake, which rewards the staking / locking of funds (like NXT or DASH), or the more common Proof of Work (used for Bitcoin), ZooBC's Proof of Participation uses a federation of nodes managed with decentralized rules. Nobody has a voice on how these nodes are added to, or ejected from, this federation.

So, without a central person to admit new people into the blockchain registry, or without an ICO or an ITO, Roberto and Barton came up with a different kind of fundraising... an INO.

Blockchain Zoo was the first to ever offer an INO. That is an initial node offering, which was an honest, democratized way to get early benefits while ensuring widespread decentralization. Using a node registry, the afore-mentioned nodes federation, members with accounts pre-registered in the genesis block (the first block of a blockchain, pre-set and included in the code node software) are allowed to create blocks from day zero. after the initial 3 months of rewards exclusive to the nodes with accounts in the genesis block, only a few new nodes will be able to join the registry each day. For each of them to join the registry, there is the need to put on hold some amount of ZooBC tokens, to earn priority on the queue of prospective new nodes. After that, depending on the quality of the node activity (their blockchain participation), their trustworthiness would be rated and rewarded accordingly.

This gave the people starting on day zero the opportunity to be among the first in the blockchain, in that federation of nodes. They would then have the best opportunity to collect all the new tokens generated by the blockchain, as part of its average course of operations.

Archival Nodes

When users run ZooBC nodes, they can do so in the smallest devices, as ZooBC nodes don't have data bloating and don't require high computation to secure the blockchain, thus they can be run at low costs. Yet, if a user decides to keep a full copy of all the data present in the blockchain, he can set up the node in a stronger machine with a large data storage system, and set his node as an archival node. This means that the node will be one of those that guarantee full access to each piece of data that has transited in ZooBC since day 1. This can be done to run statistics on all the data and to provide to the P2P network access to all the past data, when the assigned backup nodes are not available. Data can always be verified as good by recalculating its hash and matching it with the one in possession by the requestor.

1.bcz.bz/83
Interact

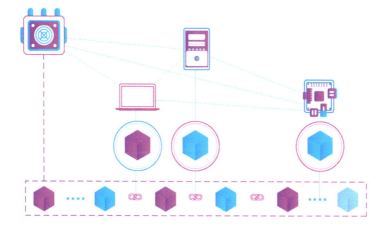

Although we leave open the possibility, via spine blocks, for casual nodes to accelerate to a recent database snapshot, never having previously downloaded or validated the chain, some node operators may wish to run a node that builds the entire chain history from scratch and maintains all data as a source for other nodes to download from.

To facilitate this, we allow a node to be configured as an archival node. In this configuration, the node will download and verify the entire history of the blockchain and will retain all blocks, transactions, receipts, and other data as a download source for other nodes.

This is not only a service to all the other nodes in the network, but may be a necessity for centralized services that need to run queries on the full history of the database, such as block explorer websites, or services to produce statistics or summaries of data in the blockchain. Any data provided by an archival node can be verified against the code ZooBC blockchain just by jumping to the needed transaction using the spine blocks as a shortcut.

While ZooBC uses a distributed file storage strategy to enable any node on the network to recover past data from its regular peers, there is always the possibility of a catastrophic failure where all nodes maintaining redundant copies of some chunk go offline simultaneously. A few people maintaining archival nodes help mitigate the risk, as the network can then recover the lost pieces. There are many reasons for people to operate archival nodes without an explicit reward mechanism, such as operating blockchain explorer applications or other applications which need a complete historical index of the data.

1.bcz.bz/87
Interact

The Humans
of Blockchain Zoo

1.bcz.bz/4v
Interact

Scan to discuss this
chapter online

Working at a great place is not just inspiring but also sustainable. Not sustainable in the 'solar panels and recycling' kind of way, but more in the way that it keeps good workers from leaving and inspires others to join. It could even be said that the modern version of "behind every great man, there is a great woman" would now be "behind every great company, there is a great team".

In the beginning, Blockchain Zoo was just an idea between a few cypherpunks, with a dream.

However, these were not your run-of-the-mill blockchain and decentralized tech enthusiasts. The founder and CEO of Blockchain Zoo, Roberto Capodieci, was already a renowned figure in blockchain, after his time spent in the NXT Foundation. Other crypto projects he was involved with included DeBuNe, OT Docs, and MagniSign. His partnership with co-founder and CTO Barton Johnston, a crypto, AI, and decentralized tech whiz from Texas, was an ideal fit for the company.

In early 2019, of the 9 initial co-founders, the only ones working full time at Blockchain Zoo were Barton, Roberto, and Stefano. In March, Stefano flew from Italy to Thailand to meet the other two. Roberto was already there for a friend's wedding, while Barton had just flown in from Bali. This was followed by 10 days of intense brainstorming, bonding, and nightlife partying (though not too late, as these were still three geeky guys more comfortable going over crypto concepts than staying up till 6 am, drinking Mai Tais).

Every morning, they headed to a local coffee shop with their laptops, so they could talk shop. This meant discussing ideas, coding proofs of said ideas, experimenting with new concepts, and writing annotations that would be helpful down the road, as the concepts were further built. (It's worth mentioning that this book was directly influenced by those notes.) The three of them eventually went to Bali to work with their top developers, ready to get the project off the ground.

As the developers understood what was to be achieved, they were inspired and immediately went to code. The first results were early prototypes for each part of this novel method to secure blockchains, which both Roberto and Barton had envisioned, with Stefano, in Thailand. The rest of Blockchain Zoo's developers were working to deliver the last two big projects for a big client.

These projects were helping finance the growing expenses of the young company, but the client, unfortunately, closed their offices right before final delivery, with a large amount of unpaid work. Although the timeframe to build the blockchain platform had just been decidedly shortened — from an earlier 'mid-2021' stable version release — it still had a "blessing in disguise" effect.

Thanks to the cancellation of the other projects, Blockchain Zoo suddenly had 23 more premium developers with the right company culture, skills, and know-how, who were ready to work on the new project! So from April 2019 onwards, this became the only project Blockchain Zoo was working on. This happened not just on the technical side, but the branding team also started documenting the evolution of the project, behind the scenes of the work that was being done.

A few months later, after various rounds of names, one suggested by Barton became the project's name: ZooBC. Other options like the "Zoo Chain", the "ZooBlockchain", or even "Blockchain Zoo's Blockchain" were thrown around. But ZooBC (which is not an animal exposition happening before the birth of Christ) was short, effective, and to the point. The URL ZooBC.com was also available — so it was immediately registered and the designers started working on the logo.

The only way the phrase "behind every great company, there is a great team" works is if it has willful, visionary leadership, ready to step up when things get tough. This was proven by walking the walk when two of the co-founders, with the help of one more shareholder, covered the $600k loss that Blockchain Zoo had, to restore the runway and bring this project to success.

Constants

While we have described in general terms the behavior of the new systems and algorithms we have developed, many of the hard numbers and constants which will be deployed in the full release of ZooBC have not yet been determined. During our alpha and beta testing phases we will continue to reason about the best values for these parameters. Some of the major sets of constants are described below.

1.bcz.bz/88
Interact

Tokens

The total amount of tokens that will ever be produced by ZooBC (token cap). We will evaluate technical considerations like fungibility and psychological considerations to arrive at what we feel is the best total token supply.

1.bcz.bz/89
Interact

https://blogchainzoo.com/glossary/z/zoo/

https://blogchainzoo.com/glossary/z/zoobit/

Coinbase

The rate at which new tokens are created by the network, the curve describing how this number will change with time, and how long it will take to generate and distribute them all. We aim to reward early network participants more than later ones to incentivize early participation, while ensuring the rewards will still be sufficient to incentivize node operators for decades.

1.bcz.bz/8a
Interact

Participation Score

The score earned or lost by a node when publishing receipts, finding blocks, etc., and its default initial score when entering the node registry. This will influence how difficult it is for nodes to rise or fall in score, which consequently influences how easy it is to maximize your rewards or to be kicked out from the registry.

1.bcz.bz/8b
Interact

 VIDEO

Relation of
Participation
and Rewards

 FORUM

Join Discussions
about Participation
Score

 ZOOBC Q&A

Get Your Questions
about Participation
Answered

Get Your Questions
about Rewards
Answered

Total Number of Nodes

The number of nodes we aim to register in the genesis block of the network, along with the maximum registry size (if any) and the rules governing the rate at which nodes are added from the queue. We aim to allow new nodes to join as quickly as we find to be secure with the Proof of Participation algorithm.

1.bcz.bz/8c
Interact

Assigned Peers

The number of peers from the registry each node is assigned during each network topology period. Selection of this number will be based on the number of simultaneous open connections we can expect from any given node on the network and how many maximum hops we want a transmission to take to be gossipped to all nodes in the network. Particularly, we balance minimizing the hops for a piece of data to traverse the entire network by minimizing the number of simultaneous open connections we expect any given node to have.

1.bcz.bz/8d
Interact

Block Time

The average time between blocks. We aim to reduce this as much as we can without causing forking problems, as this will make the blockchain more responsive.

1.bcz.bz/8e
Interact

 VIDEO

Block Timing
Algorithm

 ZOOBC Q&A

Get Your Questions
about Block Time
Answered

Max Transactions per Block

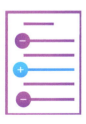

Closely related to block time, we aim to tune this number as high as we can without creating network problems, and without creating a centralizing requirement of high-powered computers to run nodes.

1.bcz.bz/8f
Interact

Receipt Filters

Receipt filtering involves several parameters, including how tightly to restrict the data filter, how to compute the expiry time from the network size, the number of assigned peers, etc. If these filters are too restrictive, honest nodes will see their participation score fall unfairly, but if they are too wide, nodes will have room to skip participation or form attacking groups without being punished. Through testing we will refine each of these numbers until the network operates smoothly and securely.

1.bcz.bz/8g
Interact

Receipt Batch Size

The number of receipts which are used to generate each receipt Merkle root. In tuning this parameter, we aim to maximize the number of receipts which can be proven by any given Merkle root, while minimizing the time between a receipt being collected and being proven on the network.

1.bcz.bz/8h
Interact

State Pruning

Which pieces of data can safely be removed from state snapshots, and how long should they, and other items such as old unused accounts, be retained How to calculate the fee for a piece of data to be posted so that it survives pruning for a long time. We aim to minimize the size of the state without losing any valuable information.

1.bcz.bz/8j
Interact

Attack Vectors

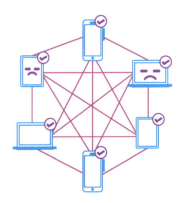

A decentralized technology is only as useful as its resistance to attacks from malicious actors. We have developed several theories of attack against the protocol we propose here, many of which have been mentioned in the sections where they apply.

In this section, in a later version of this paper, we will list and analyze all possible attack vectors on ZooBC. Blockchain Zoo will hire white hat hackers to attempt attacks, as well as offer bounties for users demonstrating an attack on ZooBC. Additionally, we will perform attacks against our own test networks and collect the results.

As we continue to refine the protocol and gather data from our alpha and beta testing phases, and collect feedback from the community, we will create a detailed accounting of possible attack vectors, how we have simulated them, and any measurements we have made demonstrating the security of the protocol.

1.bcz.bz/8k
Interact

ZooBC Tools

Wallet

 VIDEO

 How to Use the ZooBC Wallet

 Wallet Features

 What Makes the ZooBC Wallet Unique?

 FORUM

 Join Discussions about 3rd Party Clones and Wallets

 Join Discussions about Wallets Developed by ZooBC

 ZOOBC Q&A

 Get Your Questions about Wallets Answered

How to get some ZBC testnet tokens to play with ZooBC

At the moment, we have decided not to publish a public testnet faucet. During the alpha and beta releases of ZooBC, there will be chain resets (the blockchain is rebooted to accommodate changes to the protocol) leaving users suddenly with an empty wallet. To make it easier to trace who already had received testnet tokens and who received them before a chain reset, and to warn users of testnet chain resets, we are giving testnet tokens to the community support team.

1.bcz.bz/3m
Interact

Request ZBC testnet tokens via:

- Feedback function in the mobile or desktop wallet
- Forum - Token thread
- Telegram group

Mobile Wallet

ZooBC team is implementing Android and iOS mobile wallets, structuring the code to make it easy for integrations and custom implementation. The mobile wallet includes a DApps section, where the UI for DApps can be loaded for seamless interaction of the user with the app. The mobile wallet integrates with hardware wallets allowing the user to secure private keys outside the mobile phone.

1.bcz.bz/8r
Interact

Download the iOS and Android alpha version of the ZooBC mobile wallet.

Participate in ZooBC Mobile Wallet Testing

The Android version is available during the alpha and beta versions of ZooBC. It is not available in the Play Store. The iOS Alpha version has been released with TestFlight (an iPhone app to test applications before they are put online in the App Store). At the time of release of the beta version of ZooBC, in the TestNet, both Android and iOS versions will be published in the relative app stores.

Send us your feedback with ideas, suggestions, or bug reports.

Web Wallet

ZooBC also has a default web wallet to allow users to access their core account data and functionalities from the web. The web wallet allows nodes owners to interact with all the functionalities needed to manage and monitor blockchain nodes. Also, the web wallet is being implemented to load specific DApps UI and to accept signatures made with hardware wallets and government-released IDs.

1.bcz.bz/8t
Interact

Go to the ZooBC desktop wallet

▷ VIDEO

Node Registration
in the Web Wallet

How Can a User
Register the Node?

Participate in ZooBC Desktop Wallet Testing

The alpha version of the web wallet is online and connects to the alpha TestNet. Use either the mobile or the web wallet to generate your account address. Request demo tokens (testnet ZBC) to try the wallet using the feedback button. NOTE: many functionalities have not been implemented yet in the wallet, some aren't yet in the node app. Several "coming soon" functions show what will be available in the near future.

Send us your feedback with ideas, suggestions, or bug reports.

Key Management

Digital signatures, a core part of how a user interacts with a blockchain, require the management of seed phrases and private keys. If a user loses or forgets his seed words or his private key, he loses access to its blockchain account and nobody can provide help to recover the account. Most web wallets offer the possibility to store an encrypted seed phrase in a centralized server, that the user can download and decrypt to restore his access to the account. Other web wallets offer multisig accounts, where 2 out of 3 signatures are necessary to execute transactions. The user holds two, and the web wallet holds one. This offers security as the web wallet cannot execute transactions alone, the user can, and the web wallet exists as a spare key in case the user loses one of the two he has. ZooBC is working to offer innovative key management to allow users to safely store their keys and restore access to their accounts when needed.

1.bcz.bz/8u
Interact

▷ **VIDEO**

What Is the ZooBC Key
Management Feature?

Block Explorer

Blockchain Zoo is working on a block explorer system, made of a server-side application and a web UI interface, to offer visualization of blockchain data from the basic ones such as blocks and transactions, to data specific to the Proof of Participation protocol. This tool can be customized to highlight specific DApp's state and be deployed by anyone that needs to offer to their users a specific frontend to monitor pieces of information particulat to their application.

1.bcz.bz/8v
Interact

Explore the live blockchain: https://zoobc.net

FORUM

 How to Install the Explorer on a MacOS

 Join Discussions about Explorer

 Join Discussions Related to the Explorer

ZOOBC Q&A

 Get Your Questions about Explorer Answered

Participate in ZooBC Explorer Testing

Like every blockchain, ZooBC also has a block explorer. It is a work in progress, but you can use the alpha version of the block explorer to monitor the transactions you send and receive, and the overall transactions sent in the blockchain. As ZooBC has a very unique way of working, due to the use of Proof of Participation, the block explorer also shows details that are specific to this protocol. If you have feedback or a question, if you have ideas on what the block explorer should visualize, if you feel something isn't working properly... send us your feedback!

 Explore the live blockchain: https://zoobc.net

Blockchain Zoo: The End
of the Beginning

1.bcz.bz/4x
Interact

Scan to discuss this
chapter online

Overcoming challenges is what life is all about. Like a great epic, the Blockchain Zoo story also involves seemingly-impossible challenges, as well as interesting characters, occasional conflict, lessons learned, journeys across exotic places, successes, and even a wedding and a new baby!

It's a story that continues well into 2021, with the soon-to-be-released early version of the blockchain, ZooBC. Since it has its very own consensus model — Proof of Participation, or PoP — it went through various stages of development, until the first stable version could be released.

ZooBC's PoP was carefully considered, planned, and built as a trusted peer-to-peer network of nodes, allowing access to its blockchain federation slowly and sustainably. It replaces the use of coin/token value, in order to safeguard the chain with useful work (a user's participation) to keep the network alive. Examples might be government offices around a country seeking safe data encryption and sharing within a blockchain, or a consortium of hospitals that wants to manage medical records securely in a decentralized manner, as part of a strong network, without the need to worry about a token value.

Alongside the ZooBC release, the behind-the-scenes work of dozens of talented developers, the marketing team, and leadership, will also begin to pay off, as the project gains prominence in the blockchain space. This includes the documentation of the project's evolution, that ultimately were incorporated into the book you are reading right now, to explain the ZooBC story and technology in more detail.

Another element of classic stories is that of the unexpected (or reluctant) hero: the humble farmer who is fated to change the world, against all odds. The soldier who wants nothing more than to have peace but must instead fight a war against his own empire.

The princess who rises above her parents' strict wishes, so she can pursue her dreams... and so on. The Blockchain Zoo team members also unexpectedly found themselves in a place they didn't know the company would be in.

From 2017 to early 2019, Blockchain Zoo had spent its formative years building custom blockchains for other clients. Among a variety of services, we created special transaction types, customized consensus rules, and more. Throughout that time, the team listed all the different pain points they would have loved to see addressed on an ideal blockchain platform... So they built it.

What makes ZooBC special?

Just creating one innovation wouldn't be enough. The blockchain space moves so fast, with so many ambitious players, that if the team wanted to be successful, they needed to develop several innovations, with all components working well together. Some of these ZooBC innovations include:

- **Compliance**
  - Transactions can be signed with government-issued digital signatures
  - Accounts can refuse/accept incoming transactions

- **Native Blockchain Objects (Digital Twins: Items with Editable Data and Properties)**
  - Accounts can create blockchain objects
  - Blockchain objects can change ownership, be transferred, updated, sold, etc.

- **Native Escrowed Transactions**
  - Automated with centralized services (easily creates a decentralized exchange)
  - Human managed (for example the execution of a title transfer can be authorized by a notary)

- **Native Cryptographic Multisig**
  - Transactions can be prepared both on-chain and off-chain
  - Multisig works hierarchically and natively with escrowed transactions

- **Native Liquid Transactions**
  - Send funds continuously (per minute / per hour) with a max total amount that can be set
  - The transaction can be stopped by the sender, receiver, or by a 3rd party

- **Simple Code**
  - Written for everyone to customize it, well documented and easy to create with, and on top of, ZooBC

- **Snapshots**
  - Once a month the current state of the blockchain is snapshotted
  - Nodes can download snapshots and rebuild the state of the blockchain at various point in time
  - Snapshots can be cryptographically validated without downloading the whole blockchain

- **Native Distributed Data Storage**
  - NOTE: In ZooBC V1 is only used to store blocks and status snapshots
  - Data is stored in a subset of nodes, with enough redundancy, but only used for blocks and snapshots for now
  - In future versions of ZooBC, it will also be used for transaction attachments, personal storage, decentralized web hosting, etc.

- **And More, Including Spine Blocks, Quickly Running New Nodes, Scalability, and DApps.**

The future for the whole blockchain ecosystem is bright, as it is for Blockchain Zoo. Any (or all) of the above could be implemented by other blockchains and consensus mechanisms, or it could be ZooBC that leads the way, in implementing our solutions to some of the biggest pain points in the industry. Whichever way it goes it would be a happy ending, as it has been an incredible journey... so far.

Conclusion

As described in the introduction, this first version of ZooBC technology makes several extensions on earlier blockchain technology. We introduce the Proof of Participation mechanism, the mechanics of the node registry, state snapshots, spine blocks, a limited governance model for transaction fees, escrowed and liquid transactions, and many other innovations.

We have chosen our goals for this first release conservatively, especially emphasizing wide decentralization over scalability on the base layer, as we believe the censorship resistance and community ownership which come with such decentralization is the entire purpose of the technology. However, this does not mean that we don't intend the technology to scale, or be contained by any of the conventional limits of blockchain.

1.bcz.bz/8s
Interact

Towards the Future...

ZooBC is not only a technology, but a research initiative. The knowledge we accumulate in our implementation and experience operating the network, and any funds we raise to achieve these goals, will be directed towards advancing our passionate vision to create decentralized technologies to overcome the hurdles faced today in achieving widespread mainstream adoption. The exact details of this work still await our experience and design, but we can give a glimpse of the path ahead.

The node registry, especially, will serve as the backbone of a decentralized application (DApp) platform that Blockchain Zoo intends to develop in the next release of ZooBC. As each node's operator can choose which DApps to run (based on the node specifications), subsets of registered nodes will be able to host the DApps they select, and thus be rewarded for operating that particular DApp. In this way, the operator of a node in the registry not only stands to earn coinbase rewards from the greater network but also has the opportunity to earn greater rewards by supporting projects or applications built on top of ZooBC.

The security and decentralization of each DApp depends on the number of nodes running it. This will require DApp creators to include meaningful incentives in the logic of their decentralized applications, so that as many node operators as possible choose to run the DApp. This becomes a scalability solution in itself, a kind of "self-sharding", where only subsets of the full network manage data and consensus for individual decentralized applications.

At the base layer, we will provide the tools for these DApps to accept digital signatures in multiple formats, and to give user accounts control over which transactions they agree to receive. We wish to facilitate a level of government compatibility not only on the base layer but also for DApps built on the base layer, to create an ecosystem of applications which can be used to manage contracts, titles, and other "things" which may be demonstrated in a court of law.

In future versions, ZooBC will also adopt what has been developed in the field of zero-knowledge proofs, offering users and DApp developers the option to increase both the privacy and compressibility of user's transactions on the blockchain. This should be accomplished in such a way that it is compatible with the support for DApps, giving both users and DApp developers the option to use built-in zero-knowledge tools to easily enhance transactions within their own applications.

This is only a glimpse of where we would ultimately like to go. Blockchain Zoo looks forward to present, in future papers, detailed designs of these and other mechanisms in the next versions of the ZooBC technology and, with the support of the community, fully implemented technologies to the community.

All of us who used FidoNet, Torrent, and then Bitcoin witnessed the first sparks of a decentralized future, and many of us are now engaged in a community effort to fan those sparks into a flame which is transforming the entire information technology space. Blockchain Zoo, through its continuing efforts on the ZooBC project, seeks to attract the right minds, resources and experience, and organize them to push the cutting edge of decentralization, allowing all users to interact directly with each other and removing dependence on central intermediaries. This was the vision of Satoshi Nakamoto, and we proudly endeavor to carry forward the torch.

1.bcz.bz/8x
Interact

Learn More about ZooBC

For its growth, adoption, and strength, ZooBC relies on its community. Blockchain Zoo (the company behind ZooBC) makes a great effort to support the ZooBC community.

Please join our Blockchain Community

ZooBC Forum. The central place of the ZooBC community. Users, from the geekiest supporters to the less tech-savvy, earn a participation score and gain access as they use the forum.

Read and join ZooBC forum

ZooBC Knowledge Base. Here anyone can ask questions about ZooBC and, once a supporter becomes an expert, can answer questions posted by other community members!

Visit the ZooBC Q&A website

Support ZooBC

Bounties and Rewards

As we publish this book {1st of February 2021} the ZooBC MainNet is about to be launched. The investment made by Blockchain Zoo, and some more private money, has already surpassed the sum of USD 2 million. Unlike other crypto projects that do ICOs, we didn't want to raise funds before having a solid product to offer, and thus created ZooBC by investing our own resources. We have put together a paid team that reached almost 60 devoted software and brand developers, but at the beginning of 2021 we had to resize the team to the essential amount of 37 people.

Want to help ZooBC grow above Version 1? We have open-sourced the code of all our work under the MIT and GPL3 licenses, and it is available at https://github.com/zoobc for anyone who wants to join the team and get bounties to help with the development. For those of you who want to help, but have no development skills, we are happy to receive donations in BTC and ETH (and even via TT to our bank account) to finance the bounties for the open source community. You should read, and why not help with, our yellow paper: https://bcz.bz/yellowpaper

Blockchain Zoo will act as the foundation for the ZooBC project. You can contact us with any questions you may have at info@blockchainzoo.com and help us by donating at the following addresses:

To support ZooBC you can donate at the addresses as specified on the ZooBC.com website

BTC
bc1qzunaa59lm66kq70dt5qjeks89s6xhmu24kayuy

ETH
0xB0431975c291EC575A069654ba0f39C33222155c

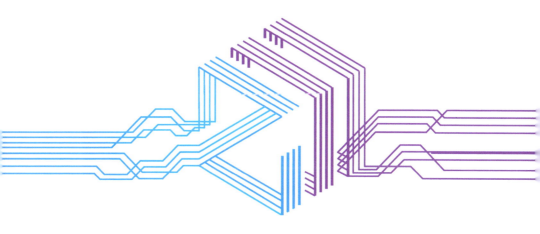

Blockchain Zoo - The ZooBC Team

"A decentralized system is one where multiple parties make their own independent decisions, and all end up moving in the same direction."

APPENDIX 1 - White Paper Older Versions

Version 1.0

Download the (clean) V1.0 of the white paper in PDF version here:

https://zoobc.com/ZooBC%20Whitepaper%20V1.0.pdf

The above V1.0 of the white paper in PDF format has a blockchain proof of existence record:

https://proofofexistence.com/detail/897842dea01bc7d128b e2bee1798020029ed6ef22101cd345b895fc80ec15cac

Version 0.2

Download the (clean) V0.2 of the white paper in PDF version here:

https://zoobc.com/ZooBC%20Whitepaper%20Draft%20 -%20V0.2.pdf

The above V0.2 of the white paper in PDF format has a blockchain proof of existence record:

*https://proofofexistence.com/detail/8a3b56fd764998e982
81506334188da469b70cf9c83968d11df1f2214f307e3f*

Version 0.1

Download the (clean) V0.1 of the white paper in PDF version here:

*https://zoobc.com/ZooBC%20Whitepaper%20Draft%20
-%20V0.1.pdf*

The above V0.1 of the white paper in PDF format has a blockchain proof of existence record:

*https://proofofexistence.com/detail/6a0cd36328a36cd8e7
44435a5b92890ba9134962f40f9165a4c15ff888fcad3e*

APPENDIX 2 - Privacy Considerations

Moving into the future of Blockchain and decentralized systems, there is increasing concern over the entirely-public nature of the data on the blockchain. While these concerns are not addressed in ZooBC V1, they stand out clearly in our minds as important to address in the technology as a whole, and so here we list the thoughts that are guiding us as we begin designing V2 of the ZooBC blockchain technology.

1.bcz.bz/8m
Interact

Data Privacy

ZooBC is implementing and will implement various aspects devoted to data privacy using zero-knowledge proof (ZKP) as a cryptographic method to allow a user (the prover) to prove to another user (the verifier) that they have the possession of some information without revealing the information to the verifier.

This is important to keep the privacy of data exposed to the network and allow the use of decentralized applications when managing data that should not be revealed to the public. As ZooBC also offers distributed storage of data (initially used to store the blockchain and the chain snapshots, but later used also to save large data payload of blockchain transactions and in subsets of nodes also decentralized apps datasets), the aspects of data privacy are a key factor for the adoption of the ZooBC blockchain platform in industries that must comply with regulatory requirements and yet need to adopt decentralized systems to ease the business processes when working with suppliers and clients.

1.bcz.bz/8n
Interact

User Privacy

With the adoption of the **GDPR (General Data Protection Regulation)** in the **European Union,** questions regarding blockchain's compliance with the act have arisen. Personal data is "any information relating to an identified or identifiable natural person". Given that identities on a blockchain are associated with an individual's public and private keys, this may fall under the category of personal data. A key part of the GDPR lies in a citizen's right to be forgotten, or data erasure. Due to the blockchain's nature of immutability, potential complications exist if an individual who made transactions on the blockchain requests their data to be deleted. ZooBC is also working to address this aspect of user privacy.

1.bcz.bz/8p
Interact

Anonymity

ZooBC aims to provide the essential tools for both systems and users that need full anonymity and applications and users that require defined identities for the users. Also, even for systems that need to identify users, there may be a need for anonymous transactions, anonymous voting, etc. ZooBC aims to use zero-knowledge-proof transactions to allow anonymous transactions, anonymous interaction with decentralized apps, and most importantly, anonymous voting where a vote per registered user is guaranteed by the system, yet what the user has voted remains anonymous.

1.bcz.bz/8q
Interact

APPENDIX 3 - Glossary

This whitepaper uses some terms or expressions that require some background knowledge of blockchain. Here is a glossary to clarify some basic terms which may ease understanding of the whitepaper:

 **Node** (also referred to as "blockchain node", "network server", "peer"): a node is a computer or server that is running the ZooBC node software. More importantly, it is connected to other nodes, running the same software, to create a network.

 https://blogchainzoo.com/glossary/n/node

Network (also referred to as "P2P", "peer to peer", "the blockchain"): A peer-to-peer network that distributes computing tasks among many private computers (decentralized servers), instead of using company computers (centralized servers).

 https://blogchainzoo.com/glossary/p/peer-to-peer-p2p

Transaction (also referred to as "payment", "transfer"): a transaction is a set of instructions that a blockchain user prepares and signs in a client application. The user then broadcasts the transaction to the network. Nodes in the network receive the transaction, execute it, and incorporate it with others into a block.

 https://en.bitcoin.it/wiki/Transaction

Fee (also referred to as "transaction fee"): the payment a user grants to the network to include her transaction in the blockchain. To submit a transaction a user needs to add a fee that is given as an incentive to nodes to maintain the blockchain. The fee is usually attached to the transaction itself; if the transaction is rejected the fee is usually returned to the user. Fees also serve as a deterrent to users from spamming or otherwise abusing a blockchain. Quote: "Ah, if only spammers had to pay a fee to send us emails..."

 https://blogchainzoo.com/glossary/t/transaction-fee

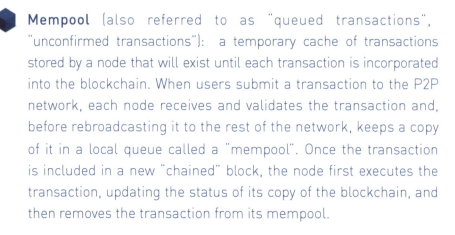

Mempool (also referred to as "queued transactions", "unconfirmed transactions"): a temporary cache of transactions stored by a node that will exist until each transaction is incorporated into the blockchain. When users submit a transaction to the P2P network, each node receives and validates the transaction and, before rebroadcasting it to the rest of the network, keeps a copy of it in a local queue called a "mempool". Once the transaction is included in a new "chained" block, the node first executes the transaction, updating the status of its copy of the blockchain, and then removes the transaction from its mempool.

https://blog.kaiko.com/an-in-depth-guide-in-to-how-the-mempool-works-c758b781c608

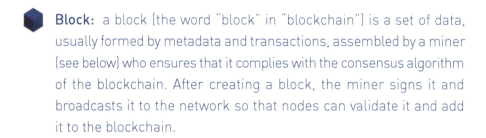

Block: a block (the word "block" in "blockchain") is a set of data, usually formed by metadata and transactions, assembled by a miner (see below) who ensures that it complies with the consensus algorithm of the blockchain. After creating a block, the miner signs it and broadcasts it to the network so that nodes can validate it and add it to the blockchain.

https://en.wikipedia.org/wiki/Blockchain#Blocks

https://blogchainzoo.com/glossary/b/block

Block Height (also referred to as "height", "blockchain height"): the position (height) of a block in the blockchain. A blockchain is composed of a sequence of unique blocks chained to one another, with each block given a sequential incremental value that determines its position in the blockchain. Each block is assigned a "height" starting from zero. The blockchain height is the total number of blocks on a blockchain.

 https://blogchainzoo.com/glossary/b/block-heigh

 Miners (also referred as "forgers", "minters", "block creators", "blocksmiths"): the accounts, in a blockchain, that, through a node, create, sign, and propose new blocks to the network. Usually, miners collect the fees of the transactions included in the blocks they create. In some blockchains, they also collect an additional reward made of new coins created with the block (see "coinbase"). In Proof of Work, an account can be owned by an individual user, or by a group of users pooling their computing resources (a "mining pool") to increase their chances of earning fees.

 https://blogchainzoo.com/glossary/m/miner

https://blogchainzoo.com/glossary/m/miner

Coinbase (also referred to as "reward", "new coins", "new tokens"): the "sender" of a special transaction included in every new block (on some blockchains) that creates new tokens from nothing. These tokens are given as a reward to the miner that creates the new block, thereby increasing the total amount of tokens in circulation within the blockchain. Some blockchains use the coinbase only at block 0 and have 100% of their tokens already created when the block-chain is launched. ("Coinbase" should not be confused with the crypto-currency exchange from San Francisco of the same name.)

https://en.bitcoin.it/wiki/Coinbase

Hashing Power (also referred to as "hashrate", "h/s", "work"): the total computing power used to calculate hashes in a Proof of Work blockchain. To make a new block valid to be broadcast to the network, miners of blockchains that use Proof of Work are required to find, through trial and error, a particular hash specific to their new block. To do so, miners purchase specialized hardware that calculates millions of hashes per second. The quantity of hashes miners can collectively produce is called hashing power.

https://en.bitcoinwiki.org/wiki/Hashrate

https://blogchainzoo.com/glossary/h/hash-rate

Blockchain (also referred to as "chain", "distributed system"):
a constantly growing list of data blocks, each containing users' transactions. Blocks are "chained" one to the other using cryptography. The "chaining" is done by adding to each new block a unique finger print (a cryptographic hash) of the previous block. How this unique fingerprint is generated is the core aspect of the mechanics that secure a blockchain (Proof of Work, Proof of Stake, or many other "Proof of..." that are used).

https://blogchainzoo.com/glossary/b/blockchain

Public / Private: Permissionless / Permissioned: different types of blockchain. A blockchain can be deployed publicly (openly accessible from the Internet) or privately (inside an access-protected Virtual Private Network, or VPN). Blockchains can also be permissionless (where a user does not need to be "authorized" to submit transactions, run nodes, etc), or permissioned (where an administrator must authorize a user's account before she can post transactions, etc.) When deploying a new blockchain, or a clone of an existing blockchain, the choice must be made to make the new blockchain public or private and permissioned or permissionless.

Public

https://blogchainzoo.com/glossary/p/public-blockchain/

Private

https://blogchainzoo.com/glossary/p/private-blockchain/

Permissioned

https://blogchainzoo.com/glossary/p/permis-sioned-ledger/

Permissionless

https://blogchainzoo.com/glossary/u/unper-missioned-ledger/

Fork (also referred to as "blockchain split", "alternative chain"): a fork occurs, like a fork in the road, when different sets of nodes in a blockchain disagree over which is a legitimate new block and create alternative versions of the chain. Most often a fork has a higher score and gets used by all nodes (see "Longest Chain", below.) A fork can be deliberate, or accidental. Between the deliberate ones there are "soft" forks and "hard" forks. A soft fork is a change in a blockchain protocol that is backward-compatible. That means that non-updated nodes are still able to process transactions and push new blocks to the blockchain, provide they don't break the new protocol rules. A hard fork is a change in a blockchain protocol that is incompatible with the previous versions, meaning that nodes that don't update to the new version won't be able to process transactions or push new blocks to the blockchain.

https://en.wikipedia.org/wiki/Fork_(blockchain)

https://blogchainzoo.com/glossary/f/fork

Longest Chain (also referred to as "highest difficulty chain", "authoritative chain"): the chain of blocks that prevails in the case of a fork (see "Fork", above.) When miners "chain" a new block to the previous one, the way th e blocks are "chained" has a value. The harder the work done in chaining a block (in PoW blockchains), or the closest a block complies to the consensus rules, the higher the score is for that piece of the chain. In the event of a fork, when a node has more than one new block or blockchain to choose from to update itself, the node calculates the cumulative "score" generated when creating each chain and chooses the chain with the highest score (in Proof of Work this "score" is referred to as "difficulty", and the chain with the highest cumulative difficulty is the chosen one). In this way, nodes in a P2P network can reach the same decision without communicating with each other, but simply using the same algorithm to evaluate the options presented to them.

https://zdl-crypto.fandom.com/wiki/Longest_Chain

Proof of... (also referred to as "consensus algorithm/mechanism /model"): a set of rules to reach a consensus in a blockchain that allows nodes to "chain" blocks to one another by evaluating the validity of transactions and the "score" of new proposed blocks. In each blockchain, nodes "prove" the validity of a transaction and a block using the same method, but many different blockchains can use different methods: the various consensus algorithms that are named "proof of..." followed by a single word describing the method (work, stake, capacity, etc.)

https://blogchainzoo.com/glossary/c/consensus -algorithm

Receipt (specific to Proof of Participation in ZooBC): a node's acknowledgment of receiving data from another node, giving evidence of the latter's participation in the network. To measure its participation in ZooBC, when exchanging information in the peer to peer network, a node acknowledges having received information from another node by sending back a digitally signed receipt. Once a node has collected enough receipts, and when it is its turn to create a block, it can include in the metadata of the block a subset of the receipts it has collected. This can be later used to prove, at consensus level, that the node has participated in the network, thus earning a participation "score".

  https://blogchainzoo.com/glossary/r/receipt

 Token (also referred to as "coin", "crypto token", "cryptocurrency", "digital assets"): a unit of value within a blockchain system, at times used as an internal currency to pay for goods and services, but essentially needed to pay the transaction fees. The financial value of tokens is determined by their current market value, which in turn depends on the level of users' trust in the blockchain.

  https://blogchainzoo.com/glossary/t/token

Stake (also referred to as "locked funds", "total deposit", "locked balance"): a user's funds that are locked or held as a guarantee. Mostly referred to in "Proof of Stake" blockchain, the stake is the economic purpose to provably commit to a promise that the user won't sell the staked tokens for a pre-established period of time.

https://medium.com/coinmonks/understanding -proof-of-stake-the-nothing-at-stake-theory- 1f0d71bc027

Address (also referred to as "account", "wallet"): an address is an alphanumeric string of that is unique to an "account". It is used to provide a digital identity (which can remain anonymous) to identify a sender or a recipient of blockchain transactions (for example, to route digital assets across the network to a particular recipient).

https://blogchainzoo.com/glossary/a/address

Address Type (also referred to as "account type", "wallet type"): addresses are the result of a particular mathematical algorithm. From a "private" key, which is secret to the user, a "public" key is calculated and from there the address the user can share with others. Government IDs and various blockchains have their own address formats. While different blockchains have unique address formats, ZooBC supports many different types of addresses in a single blockchain.

 https://unblock.net/what-is-a-blockchain-address

 Digital Signature (also referred to as "signature", "cryptographic signature"): Digital signatures are a cryptographic tool to sign messages and verify message signatures in order to provide proof of authenticity for blockchain transactions.

 https://blogchainzoo.com/glossary/d/digital-signature

Sybil Attack: a Sybil attack is a kind of security threat on an online system where someone tries to take over the network by creating multiple accounts, nodes, or computers. For example, a Sybil attack can take place when somebody runs multiple nodes on a blockchain network. Attackers may be able to out-vote the honest nodes on the network if they create enough fake identities (or Sybil identities). They can then refuse to receive or transmit blocks, effectively blocking other users from a network.

 https://en.wikipedia.org/wiki/Sybil_attack

 Fee Scale (also referred to as "fee multiplier", "multiplier"):
a variable number which set fees needs to be multiplied by, to give an adjusted fee amount to be paid for transactions. Operators of registered nodes on the network may take a regular vote on the appropriate multiplier, which we call the fee scale, for minimum transaction fees. This guarantees that while the value of the blockchain token may fluctuate, the fees paid for transactions remain stable against the regular currency.

 https://blogchainzoo.com/glossary/f/fee-scale

Peer Filter (also referred to as "connection table", "P2P topology"): The ordering of all nodes in the registry used to assign a set of preferred peers to each node. Each node computes its peer filter and connects to the assigned nodes. When a node publishes receipts, the receipts it is allowed to publish must come from one of its assigned peers at the time the receipt was created.

 https://blogchainzoo.com/glossary/p/peer-filter

 Rollback (also referred to as "reorganization", "reorg"): the work a node does to replace the last blocks when it realizes it is in a fork of the blockchain as it receives a new chain that's longer (i.e higher cumulative difficulty) than its current active chain. Reorganizations happen when a node realizes that what it thought was the canonical chain turned out not to be. When this happens, the blocks in the latter part of its chain (i.e. the most recent transactions) are reverted and the transactions in the newer replaced blocks are executed. All reorgs have a "depth," which is the number of blocks that were replaced, and a "length," which is the number of new blocks that did the replacing.

 https://learnmeabitcoin.com/guide/chain-reorganisation

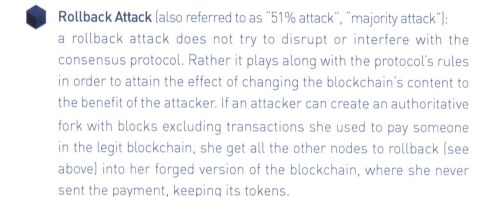

Rollback Attack (also referred to as "51% attack", "majority attack"): a rollback attack does not try to disrupt or interfere with the consensus protocol. Rather it plays along with the protocol's rules in order to attain the effect of changing the blockchain's content to the benefit of the attacker. If an attacker can create an authoritative fork with blocks excluding transactions she used to pay someone in the legit blockchain, she get all the other nodes to rollback (see above) into her forged version of the blockchain, where she never sent the payment, keeping its tokens.

https://learncryptography.com/cryptocurrency
/51-attack

Merkle Tree (also referred to as "hash tree"): a Merkle tree is just an efficient way to prove that something is in a set, without having to store the set. Merkle trees are a fundamental part of blockchain technology. A Merkle tree is a structure that allows for efficient and secure verification of content in a large body of data. This structure helps verify the consistency and content of the data.

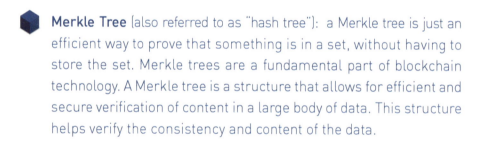

https://learncryptography.com/cryptocurrency
/51-attack

Merkle Root (also referred to as "Merkle proof"): the Merkle root is the hash of all the hashes of a set of data. In a blockchain block, all of the transaction hashes in the block are themselves hashed (sometimes several times - the exact process is complex), and the result is the Merkle root. The Merkle root, part of the block header, is the hash of all the hashes of all the transactions in the block.

 https://blogchainzoo.com/glossary/m/merkle-root

 Privacy (in Blockchain) (also referred to as "zero-knowledge encryption"): Zero-knowledge encryption means that service providers know nothing about the data stored on their servers. Zero-knowledge means that no one besides the user has the keys to her data, not even the service she is storing her files with.

Also known as private encryption, it is the ultimate way in which a user can keep data private, though it does come with a few downsides: most important of these is that if the user loses the decryption key, the data is gone forever.

https://www.cloudwards.net/what-exactly-is-zero-knowledge-in-the-cloud-and-how-does-it-work

Zero-Knowledge Proof (also referred to as "anonymous transactions"): a zero-knowledge proof (ZKP) is a cryptographic method which allows one person (the prover) to prove to another person (the verifier) that they have possession of some information without revealing the information to the verifier. A zero-knowledge proof (ZKP) private transaction protocol helps accelerate the adoption of secure, private transactions over public blockchains.

 https://www.altoros.com/blog/zero-knowledge-proof-improving-privacy-for-a-blockchain

 Digital Twins (also referred to as "chain to off-chain bridge"): "Digital twins" is the phrase used to describe a computerized (or digital) version of a physical asset and/or process. The digital twin contains one or more sensors that collect data to represent real-time information about the physical asset.

 https://en.wikipedia.org/wiki/Digital_twin

Nonce (also referred to as "salt"): Nonce is an abbreviation for "number only used once." In cryptography, a nonce is an arbitrary number that may only be used once. It is often a random or pseudo -random number issued in an authentication protocol to ensure that old communications cannot be reused in replay attacks. Nonces can also be useful as initialization vectors and in the cryptographic hash function.

 https://www.investopedia.com/terms/n/nonce.asp

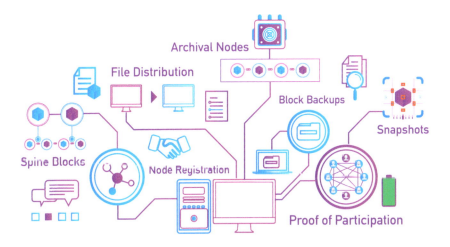

APPENDIX 4 - Consensus Algorithms

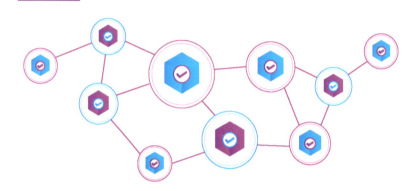

The blockchain space is saturated with attempts to improve efficiency, security, and fairness in the way that nodes reach a consensus on the history of events witnessed by the network. While the explosion of strategies may seem overwhelming or unnecessary, each project (some more than others) is doing its part in exploring the properties and tradeoffs yielded by each approach, and the crypto community is collectively narrowing down the proposed consensus strategies Darwinistically, until only the strongest are left standing.

1.bcz.bz/28
Interact

Here is a brief overview of the major approaches to blockchain consensus, and our reasoning to claim Blockchain Zoo's Proof of Participation as an improvement over its predecessors.

Proof of Work Consensus

———

The Bitcoin whitepaper introduced the concept of using accumulated "Proof of Work" as a method for any node to agree on which blockchain, among forks, should be trusted. This approach was very powerful because it allowed nodes to independently and objectively agree on one proposed history of events among many alternatives, in a way that resists a "Sybil attack" (because votes are counted by CPU cycles, not by accounts). While many insist that Proof of Work is still the safest way to secure a blockchain, time has shown some undesirable properties of the algorithm.

First, the energy usage to secure such a system is always increasing, as miners participate in an arms race to claim more of the newly generated tokens. As of 2019, Bitcoin mining consumes as much energy as the nation of Switzerland (population 8.5 million), and as the token value appreciates the energy consumed is expected to rise. Some argue the security of this approach is worth the cost, but we believe this is a less-than-ideal property.

Second, this arms race has created a condition where an individual miner with average hardware is unlikely to find a block for himself during his natural lifespan. To fairly distribute the rewards for providing hash power to the blockchain, people have resorted to "pooling" their hash power together and proportionally dividing the block reward when any of them find a block. At the time of writing, there are about 12 mining pools with a non-negligible chance to successfully add blocks to the Bitcoin history, with all others unlikely to ever meaningfully participate. This level of centralization puts the "censorship resistance" property of Bitcoin in jeopardy, as it is not difficult to imagine a condition where a government or other organization may coerce 12 pool operators into complying with its demands to censor some transactions. We believe this failure to resist the tendency toward centralization is another less-than-ideal property.

Third, Proof of Work mining does not require the consent of any participants on the network for an outside party to become dominant. If someone truly had the money and the will to buy a majority of the hash power and use it to damage the chain, they could do so, even if all other long-time network participants wished to prevent it. It is debatable whether this is a desirable property or not, as it prevents the long-time stewards of the chain from ensuring they can maintain control for themselves. We believe it is fairer to give the vote to those who maintained and protected the network, rather than to whoever has the money to accumulate hash power, and therefore we perceive this potential for externalized control to be a less-than-ideal property.

1.bcz.bz/29
Interact

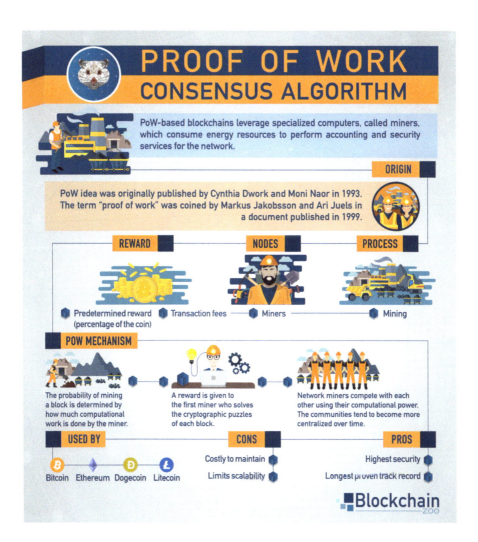

Proof of Stake Consensus

––––––

The first and third concerns described above motivated some to develop an alternate consensus algorithm to objectively choose between proposed versions of the blockchain history called "Proof of Stake". In this approach, the likelihood of a network participant to add a block to the history is computed according to how many tokens on the network she possesses, and the block she creates is proven to originate from her via a digital signature. In this way, which chain required "more work" to create is simulated by a calculation of which nodes added blocks at which times and their relative stakes. This design requires minimal energy and guarantees that, in a fork, the nodes will choose the blockchain created by the majority of highly-invested network participants -- in other words, those who have a larger stake of tokens locked to create new blocks. However, this strategy still has some undesirable properties.

First, the second concern described above regarding the centralization of mining power applies equally to Proof of Stake. When a new Proof of Stake blockchain launches, it has very often all the tokens that will ever exist "pre-mined". As a new blockchain is known by few, it is very likely that, either at the launch of the blockchain or at a later time, a majority of the tokens will be in the hands of only a few participants who can distribute them in many anonymous accounts. These few participants will create almost all of the blockchain history, as well as claim any rewards, such as the transaction fees, meant to incentivize the entire network to run nodes. If one party owns 51% of the stake, or parties who own as much decide to conspire, they can effectively censor the transactions which are accepted on the blockchain, or at a later time create an alternate history which will be accepted by the rest of the nodes.

Second, even in the event that the block-creating power is well-distributed, someone could come in possession of the private keys of accounts which, even if they are now empty, at some point in time had a large stake. Using those accounts, an attacker can create an alternate blockchain history that starts from the time those accounts had a large balance. This alternative fork may be seen, by other nodes, as the most authoritative chain, forcing them to switch to it. An attacker might purchase past private keys for less than the potential gains of creating an alternate blockchain history. Similarly, if someone discovered a vulnerability in the node software which allows private keys to be copied from the servers, they could quietly collect enough of the participants' keys to take over the blockchain. Importantly, as Proof of Work advocates note, creating an alternate chain would require only trivial energy to be invested, and so this hijacking of a Proof of Work blockchain could be performed quickly and cheaply once the necessary keys were collected.

This second concern is exacerbated by the first: the more centralized the blockchain is, the more vulnerable it is to outside manipulation. In fact, if at any point in the blockchain's history the majority of the block-creating power was controlled by only a small number of private keys, anyone who can get their hands on these few keys, even if those accounts now are empty and abandoned, can effectively re-write the blockchain history from that time forward and have it accepted by other honest nodes running the network at the time of their choosing in the future.

1.bcz.bz/2a
Interact

Federated Consensus

The first concern above can be addressed by having a fixed number of participants who each contribute to the blockchain history equally (regardless of hash power or stake), thus ensuring that network rewards and history-creating power cannot centralize to one entity. Further, the second concern can be mitigated by ensuring that the number of these participants (and therefore the number of keys that would need to conspire to create a new longest chain) is large. Consensus algorithms that embrace this theory of security are known as "federated" Consensus and have been well-studied long before the emergence of blockchain technology for use in other distributed systems. While we feel such strategies effectively address the concerns above, in other ways they are a step backward from Proof of Work and Proof of Stake.

First, federated networks are no longer "permissionless": It is no longer open for any person to simply join the network and begin participating in the consensus process, regardless of their merit or investment in the network. Usually some centralized process exists to govern which participants are admitted into, or ejected from, the federation, and this central process becomes precisely the weakness that must be avoided in truly decentralized systems, as it gives disproportionate control of the network to whoever manages the process. Some Federated Consensus models allow users to vote on who can be admitted into the federation, but this voting procedure may also be vulnerable to manipulation.

Second, this set of federated entities is usually well known (in fact, Federated Consensus strategies gain their promise of security by showing that the participants are separate well-trusted entities). This makes it easy for an external adversary to identify who needs to be pressured (technically, legally, financially, or otherwise) to censor the network. Additionally, by virtue of the fact that the participants are already connected by at least one entity (the entity which approves their membership in the federation), it is not difficult to imagine them conspiring off-chain to achieve some mutual goal.

For these reasons, we feel a pure federation is not acceptable for secure decentralized consensus, although it has some properties we would like to preserve. Proof of Authority and Proof of Reputation (based on Proof of Authority) are two examples of federated consensus algorithms.

1.bcz.bz/2b
Interact

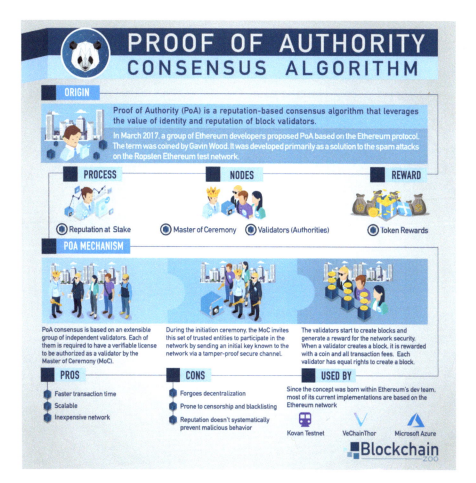

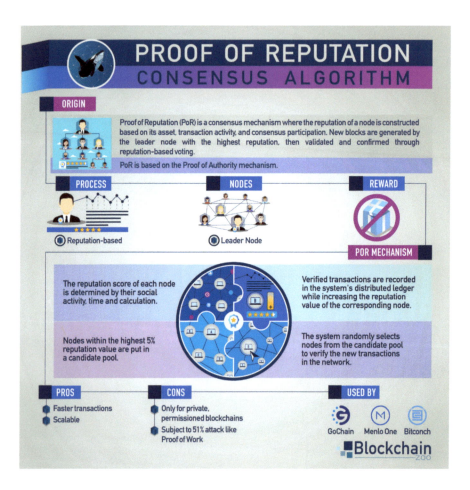

Delegated Proof of Stake Consensus

One of the most popular modern approaches to improving the scale of a blockchain network is to use "Delegated Proof of Stake" Consensus, where the accounts of the blockchain vote, with their stake, for a small number of nodes, running large enough hardware, to become block creators and thus support a high transaction volume blockchain. While this approach can dramatically increase the throughput of the network, it does so at the expense of decentralization, having similar flaws as conventional Proof of Stake and small federations (as described above). Specifically, these are the ease of quickly collecting enough stake to control the network, and the ability of a small number of block creators to conspire to censor transactions.

While recognizing the importance of creating more scalable blockchain technology, a pseudo-centralized approach is not the correct path. ZooBC aims for the technical and financial requirements of operating a node to not exceed those available to the average user, enabling a blockchain that is directly operated by a large number of small, independent actors. ZooBC offers a solution which both vastly increases the number of keys which would need to be compromised to rewrite the blockchain and makes it significantly more difficult for such actors to conspire or be coerced by an adversary seeking to censor the blockchain.

1.bcz.bz/2c
Interact

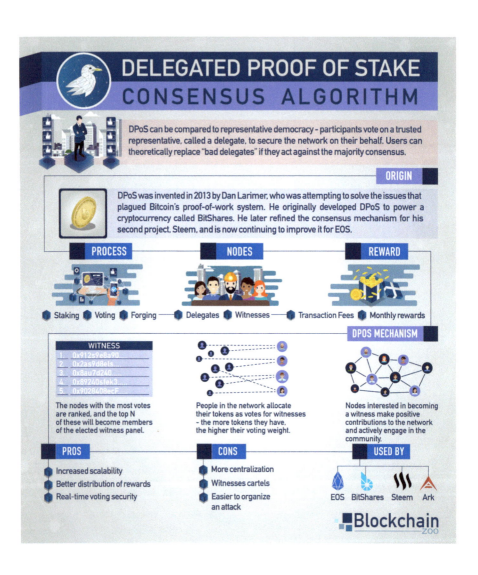

Byzantine Fault Tolerant Consensus

Another popular strategy for increasing the transaction throughput of a decentralized network is an algorithm called "Practical Byzantine Fault Tolerance". This algorithm is especially used in Federated Consensus, where the participants are pre-selected, because it carries a particular weakness in the face of Sybil attacks (when one attacker can operate many nodes on the network) which would make it unsuitable for some pBFT networks.

While the algorithm used can increase the speed of transaction processing, pBFT Consensus suffers from a particular property that cannot be tolerated: an attacker controlling as few as 1/3 (one third) of the nodes can prevent the entire network from reaching consensus. This may be a safe assumption to make in a federated network with tightly regulated members, but in a public, permissionless network, we feel this is too vulnerable to attack. For this reason ZooBC follows in the tradition of blockchains where an attacker must reliably control more than 1/2 (half) of the network (and therefore properly be the majority) in order to have a chance to control the network's behavior.

1.bcz.bz/2d
Interact

https://medium.com/codechain/why-n-3f-1-in-the-byzantine-fault-tolerance-system-c3ca6bab8fe9

Proof of Participation Consensus

––––––

Based on consideration of the various flaws and tradeoffs in the consensus mechanisms explored above, ZooBC adopts a few elements of Proof of Stake and of Federated Consensus strategies, combined with a novel algorithm developed by Blockchain Zoo to prove that a node is performing useful work for the network. We call this "Proof of Participation" consensus.

ZooBC maintains a federation of nodes that we call the "Node Registry". Only nodes within the registry are permitted to create blocks, and their probability to create the next block is more or less equal. This is similar to Federated Consensus. However, any node operator can apply for a spot in this registry, and their admittance into the registry is governed entirely by the protocol rules, not by any centralized entity. The rate at which new nodes are added to the registry is strictly limited by the protocol, and the selection of which applicants will be added is governed by how much stake they are willing to lock while they are in the registry. As nodes queue to enter the node registry, priority is given to nodes with a higher locked stake. This method uses a concept of Proof of Stake, to the extent that staking tokens (a scarce resource on the network) is used as a Sybil prevention mechanism, essential for a new blockchain.

NOTE: *The strategy of requiring nodes to lock tokens to join the "Node Registry" is applied only in the first version of ZooBC for the following reasons:*

(1) *To give a use to the token;*

(2) *To create demand for tokens;*

(3) *To reduce the tokens in circulation, thus creating scarcity;*

(4) *To limit the initial growth of the node registry;*

(5) *To prevent Sybil attacks to the newly launched blockchain.*

Future versions of ZooBC will shift from using "stake" for prioritizing access to the node registry, to participation score. The algorithm will prioritize nodes that, while in the queue, collect more participation score compared to others. This will remove the use of "stake" from ZooBC, making it a blockchain secured exclusively by participation.

Finally, when nodes in the "Node Registry" produce a block, they must include in the block some proof that they have been contributing to the network (by honestly propagating transactions and blocks). Nodes that miss their opportunity to create blocks, or which fail to include such proofs in their blocks, will gradually lose "participation score" until they are automatically removed from the registry. In this way, an operator must maintain a node that is in regular communication with the rest of the network to continue creating blocks and collecting coinbase rewards.

Coinbase rewards: as for Bitcoin, ZooBC has no "pre-mined" tokens. At the beginning of the blockchain, the total amount of tokens in existence is zero. At each block, new tokens are created and distributed to the nodes in the registry. When a new block is created, based on its block seed, a pseudo-random selection of nodes will receive new tokens. The new tokens created in the block are evenly distributed to the selected winners, but a node's probability of being selected as a winner is directly proportional to its participation score. In this way, nodes are strongly incentivized to maximize their participation score, as this also maximizes their profit on average. After enough time, all nodes which are participating reliably should reach the maximum participation score, making the distribution of new rewards between them essentially equal.

This is an element of fairness in rewards that most other blockchain technologies have not attempted to attain. For example, in Bitcoin, so long as you produce the block with the most work, no one can say whether you have been participating in other regular network activity. It is largely taken on faith that node operators are propagating blocks and transactions. In practice, this leaves much of the hard work of decentralizing the network to enthusiasts who run nodes because they care, despite their not having enough hash power or stake to ever earn rewards from the network.

This strategy resolves many of the flaws described in the previous algorithms. By virtue of using digital signatures, ZooBC avoids Proof of Work's energy consumption problem. By the use of an ever-growing federation of nodes, ZooBC equalizes the probability of each node operator to adding to the history and claiming coinbase rewards and avoids the miner centralization problem of both Proof of Work and Proof of Stake. By requiring each node to prove its participation (in the form of digitally signed messages from other nodes) ZooBC dramatically increases the number of private keys which would be needed to be compromised for an attacker to forge a longer chain, mitigating the key-stealing weakness of both Proof of Stake and Federated consensus. By allowing anyone to freely apply for a spot in the node registry, ZooBC avoids the permissioned (and therefore centralized) nature of a fully-federated network.

In the long term, this Proof of Participation strategy results in a very large pool of nodes taking turns to contribute to the network history and being equally rewarded for their service. Creating a longer chain does not only require the keys of the majority of stakeholders, but also of a majority of registered nodes in the network. To attack a PoP chain, an attacker needs to control far more than half of the nodes in the registry. Coming to possess a large majority of the registry not only requires a large investment, but also requires the time needed to have many new nodes gradually admitted into the registry, it also carries the cost of running real nodes proving their service to the network for the entire duration of the attack.

1.bcz.bz/2e
Interact

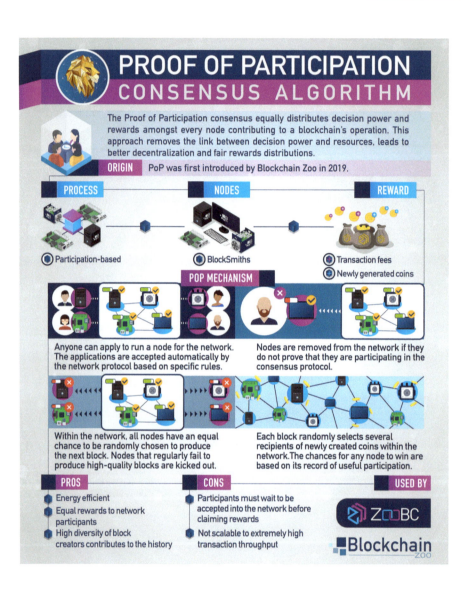

APPENDIX 5 - Websites, Groups, and Social Media

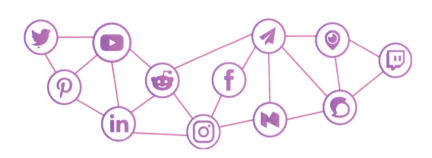

You can contribute to the discussion, ask questions, and learn more about Blockchain Zoo, ZooBC Blockchain. and BlockCoWork by visiting our websites, groups and social media channels.

◉ Website

Join our community & groups

Follow us on social media

ZooBC

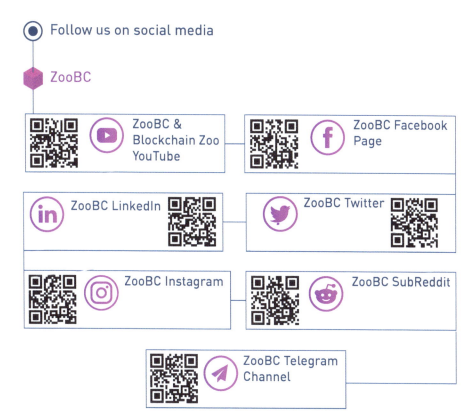

BlockCoWork

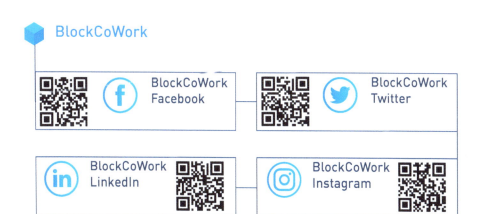

Blockchain Zoo

  Blockchain Zoo
Facebook

  Blockchain Zoo
LinkedIn

 Blockchain Zoo
Twitter

 Blockchain Zoo
Instagram

  Blockchain Zoo
Pinterest

  Blockchain Zoo
Medium

 Blockchain Zoo
Periscope

 Blockchain Zoo
Twitch

  Blockchain Zoo
Steemit

  Blockchain Zoo
Telegram
Channel

APPENDIX 6 - ZooBC Yellow Paper

We have been told that every "serious" crypto project has a "white paper", and for this reason, ZooBC should have had one. We had a lot of annotations taken during various brainstorming sessions that shaped what today is ZooBC, so we did put them together, cleaned them up, and... boom, we made this book! Cool, right? No, we still didn't have a "white paper" for ZooBC.

So we started asking ourselves: what is a "white paper"?

Here is how most dictionaries define "white paper":

White Paper, / wa t pe .p r/ in the UK, and / wa t pe .p / in the US, noun.
    1: a government report on any subject
    2: a detailed or authoritative report

The term "white paper" came about after the government color-coded reports to indicate who could access them, with the color white referring to public access. Yet, as we are not a government, the meaning we look at is the one at point 2. In the academic sense, a (white?) paper is an academic work that is usually published in an academic journal. It contains original research results or reviews existing results. Such a paper, also called an article, will only be considered valid if it undergoes a process of peer review by one or more referees, before being then published in a peer-reviewed journal.

An article is supposed to provide an overview of a topic and is usually a quite brief, while a **yellow paper** is a longer document containing research that has not yet been formally accepted or published in an academic journal. So a yellow paper, compared to an article, covers a topic in more detail, giving an in-depth view, and often includes more research.

Often research published as a white paper has also become a marketing tool that promotes a company through a sponsorship of the document itself, which is later used commercially for marketing and sales. Today's "typical" white paper is 6 to 8 pages long, but we've seen everything from a two-page flyer to a 100-page book called a "white paper."

In the crypto world, a white paper is essentially a detailed description of a project (often pushing investors to put money in an ICO). such "white papers" are no more than an authoritative report that informs readers about a complex issue and presents the issuing body's philosophy on the matter, rarely outlining an existing problem and a clear solution, and almost never giving technical information.

The "white paper" in the crypto world is essentially a flyer, or in the best cases a short document, that talks more about the financial benefits for the investors, the market reach of the project, and introduces the team behind the project.

We have put together the book you just read. That is more than enough to cover a lot of topics. So what should go in our "white" (or, after learning well the terminology, we should say "yellow") paper? What topic should it cover? How should it be written?

We decided to go ahead and try to write an academic document explaining the innovation we brought to blockchain technology: the Proof of Participation. It is a complex system, and it is not easy to explain it in detail. While it is fully clear for us (you can check the notes on the back of our napkin collection), putting it down in academic terms, with the academic methodology, is another thing.

If you are ok with reading things like this:

> Finally, when the receiver R_j has assembled these seven properties into a receipt ρ, it will compute a digital signature σ_j on the message, and attach this signature to the message, which is returned to the sender of the transmission R_i. Altogether, we may denote this receipt:
>
> $$\rho \langle R_i id, R_j id, D_{type}, D_{id}, h, B_h id, R_i \beta_h m \rangle \sigma_j$$
>
> Although, enjoying brevity, we opt for the shorter ρ in most cases, hoping that the remaining properties can be inferred from context.

then you may be a perfect candidate to help us complete the document (if you do contribute significantly we can even add your name in the people that helped). If we do a good job we then can be peer-reviewed and, who knows, be published somewhere. Maybe on the front of some napkins!

To respect the full academic standard, we have initially written the yellow paper using LaTeX technology. We used a program called TexStudio as the editor, and we had to install a big old wad of packages and applications called MacTex. Yet, today, to make life easy for you all, the yellow paper is publicly available in Google Docs, open to everyone to comment and suggest edits. You can access it simply by going to this address: http://bcz.bz/yellowpaper or by opening this QR Code:

http://bcz.bz/yellowpaper

About the Authors

Roberto Capodieci

Roberto Capodieci started in IT entrepreneurship early, selling games he coded himself in his native Italy at the age of 10, and then launching an IT company at age 14. He has been involved in decentralised systems and cryptography since torrent, and later, as peer to peer networks evolved, he engaged with blockchain. As an entrepreneur he has built several companies leveraging blockchain technology, both as a tool to manage documents, such as with Open Trade Docs and NotiFile, and on the hardware signing solutions, with ventures such as TheSoundKey and MagniSign. In 2017, he co-founded Blockchain Zoo to help the adoption of blockchain technology, consulting with many companies. It was as consultants that he and Barton Johnston realized that existing blockchain protocols were insufficient for many use cases, and decided to build their own. Roberto has so far bootstrapped ZooBC from his own funds. He lives in Bali with his wife and children.

Barton Johnston

Barton Johnston is an American who skipped college to become a programmer, releasing his first Flash game when he was 15. He has worked as a software engineer in media research, game design, home security systems, video hosting, and GPS fleet tracking, developing among others things video game lighting engines, software synthesizers for electronic music, eyegaze-tracking software for media research, and software for distributed analysis of vehicle telemetry updates. His interest in blockchain technology has focused on addressing some of its underlying technical issues, including decentralized consensus protocols, hashing, and asymmetric cryptography algorithms. He co-founded Blockchain Zoo in 2017, and after working to adapt existing blockchain protocols to clients' requirements, he realised with Roberto Capodieci that the only solution was to build afresh. He has led a software team, most of them located in Bali, to build ZooBC since March 2019. He lives in Bali with his wife.

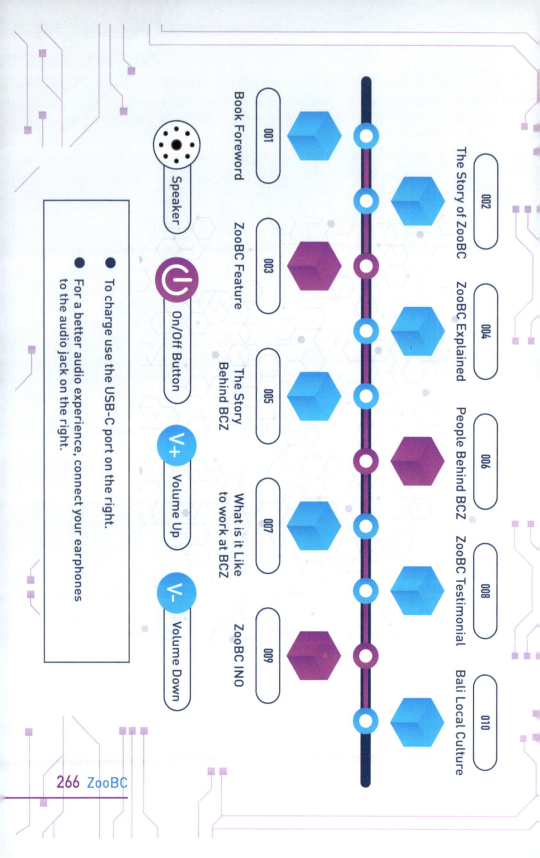

Book Foreword

001

002 The Story of ZooBC

003 ZooBC Feature

004 ZooBC Explained

The Story
Behind BCZ

005

006 People Behind BCZ

What is it Like
to work at BCZ

007

008 ZooBC Testimonial

009 ZooBC INO

010 Bali Local Culture

Speaker

On/Off Button

V+ Volume Up

V- Volume Down

- To charge use the USB-C port on the right.
- For a better audio experience, connect your earphones to the audio jack on the right.